Yes, You
Can Do This!

Yes, You Can Do This!

How Women Start Up, Scale Up, and Build the Life They Want

Claudia Reuter

WILEY

Library of Congress Cataloging-in-Publication Data:

ISBN 9781119625605 (Hardcover)
ISBN 9781119625636 (ePDF)
ISBN 9781119625629 (ePub)

Cover image: <INSERT NAME>
Cover design: <INSERT NAME>

Printed in the United States of America

10 9 8 7 6 5 4 3 2 1

To my sons, Thomas and Christopher,
who shined a light on the magic of each moment
and taught me to rethink everything.
And to Alex, for being a true partner in this journey of life.

If work, conceptualized as a career, becomes a measured line, the line often appears to be a rising one. Very often the rising career line is also, despite a residual cynicism about power, associated with a pleasant belief in the progress of the world. Even those who have refused to fit this profile know very well that they are measured against it by others who rise to the top and, from this top-of-the-career worldview, set the prevailing standards.
    —Arlie Hochschild, "Inside the Clockwork of Male Careers"

Contents

Introduction: Create the Life You Want by Starting Up   1

Moving Past the Binary Set-Up   3

A Little Background on *Lean In*   4

So Why Not Lean In by Starting Up and Move Past the
     Binary Setup?   5

The Privilege of Flexibility at Work   7

So Let's Explore Another Option: Entrepreneurship   9

Win or Lose, How Do I Know You Can Do This?   10

Why This Book Is for *You*   11

How to Read This Book   12

SECTION I: Get Ready to Start Up   15

**Chapter 1: So You Want More: Get Off the Fence,
              Start a Business, and Create the Life You Want**   17

The Monthly Mentor Gathering   17

Real-World Experiences and Opportunities   20

Entrepreneurship as the Path Forward   20

What's Holding You Back?   22

My Journey to Becoming a Startup Entrepreneur   24

What Starting Up as a Stay-at-Home Mom Looked Like   25

A Manifesto for Women to Become Entrepreneurs,
     and a Playbook to Help   28

**Chapter 2: Reasons to Lead: All the Cool Things You Can
              Do When You're in Charge**   31

A Little More About Sophie …   31

Why a Business Can Give You the Life You Want   33

You Can Change the Rules   33

The History on This Is Still Recent   36
Legislation Can't Be the Only Path Forward   36

**Chapter 3: Stop Believing Your Own Unconscious Bias:
         Develop the Mindset and Self-Confidence
         to Be the One in Charge with Gratitude**   43
Hannah at Work   43
Making the Ask   46
A Few Things About This Conversation   46
How We Think and Act Is Conditioned   47
How to Consider Unconscious Bias and Self-Advocacy
  as You Start Up   48
I Didn't Always Have This Figured Out   51
Why Affirmations Matter (Yes, You Can Is a Good Example!)   53

**Chapter 4: Your Perceived Weaknesses Are Your Hidden
         Strengths: How to Leverage Your Weaknesses
         to Start Up**   59
When It All Goes Wrong   59
Let's Role-Play!   62
You Really Are Perceived and Treated Differently   63
Goal Setting as a Framework for Success versus
  Perfectionism   64

**SECTION II: Building for Scale and Avoiding the Traps:
         Debunking the Myth That Women Don't Think
         Big Enough**   69

**Chapter 5: You Might Have the Next Big Thing:
         Your Experiences Are Different Experiences
         Than Others'**   71
Innovation Is a Broader Term than You Might Think   71
Seeing What's Possible   74
Identifying Types of Innovations   74

Why Diversity of Viewpoints in Innovation Leads to More
   Innovation   77
The Creator of Liquid Paper (White-Out)   78
An Incremental Innovative Sales Strategy That Created
   a Different Way to Sell: Tupperware   79
An Incremental Product Innovation That Created
   a Billionaire: SPANX   80
A Disruptive Business Model Innovation: Rent the Runway   81
Turning Reviews into a Viable Business Model   82
A Makeup Artist Takes on an Entire Industry   82
My Own Experience   83

Chapter 6: Build Your Confidence by Writing Down Your Future:
          How to Develop and Use a Business Plan as
          Your Personal Playbook (and to Combat Imposter
          Syndrome)   **87**
Getting Back to Sophie ...   87
Standing Up for Your Business and Fighting Imposter
   Syndrome   90
Making Your Vision Concrete   91
Developing a Business Plan   93
How My Business Plan Helped Me   97

Chapter 7: Tell a Bigger Story: Don't Apologize for
          Thinking Bold   **103**
Is Your Story Big Enough for Investors?   103
Putting the Press Release Strategy to Work   106
A Brief Example   107
Own Your Ideas with Confidence   108

Chapter 8: It Really Is Okay to Make Mistakes:
          How to Plan for Them So You Can Quickly Recover   **111**
The Others Arrive   111
How to Get Started on the Financial Plan   117

Chapter 9: You Don't Have to Wait for Revenue to Ask for Funding: Create a Compelling Pitch Deck That Gets Others on Board   **121**
Six Months Later ...   121
When Bootstrapping ...   124
Seeking Investors   127

SECTION III: Lead and Operationalize   **135**

Chapter 10: Empathy Is One of Your Biggest Assets: Use It to Understand Your Customers and Make Your Teams Stronger   **137**
As Starboard Grew   137
Creating an Environment Where People Want to Work
  Starts with Knowing People   141
Understanding Your Employees' Working Styles   142
Little Things Lead to Bigger Success   142
Working Together to Improve Outcomes and Customer
  Satisfaction   143

Chapter 11: Instill a Growth Mindset in Your Teams: Constant Change and Transitions Are Never Easy   **147**
When You Move Beyond the Startup and People Start to
  Silo into Positions   147
Building for Organizational Success through Your
  Company's Mission   149

Chapter 12: The Same Skills That Make You a Great Mom Make You a Great Manager: Bust Out Your Multitasking Skills as Your Team Grows   **153**
Sophie's Day   153
Managing the Small Corporation of Your Family   155
Being a Mom Is Being a Manager   157
Dismissing the Guilt of Being a Stay-at-Home Mom   158
How Your Two-Year-Old Honed Your Management Skills
  Like No Other   159

Chapter 13: You Are More Than Your Product or Company:
Protecting Egos When Things Change   **163**
Letting Go to Move Forward   163
Diffusing Fear and Creating Psychological Safety   164

Chapter 14: Balance Life at High Speeds: Make Time for Yourself   **167**
Running on Fumes   167
My Story (and Cautionary Tale)   169
What Balance Really Means   170

Conclusion: You Really Can Start Up and Scale a Business:
You Might Just Change the Rules in the Process   173
Sophie and Jake   173
Hannah and Stan   174
Maria and Jill   174
How Will You Start Up?   175
Overcoming the Scarcity Mindset: There's Enough
    for All of Us   176
Valuing Women as Entrepreneurs   177
Find, and Later Become, a Mentor   178

Bibliography   181

Acknowledgments   191

About the Author   193

Index   195

Introduction: Create the Life You Want by Starting Up

Shortly after the birth of my first child, I dropped out of the traditional workforce because I felt that my options were limited as a new parent and I actually wanted to be with my young child. At the time, I couldn't rationalize how spending a significant portion of my take-home salary on childcare and not seeing my new baby during the day were worth it. I had read countless books and articles on early childhood development during my pregnancy and the data on the importance of an individual caregiving experience seemed critical. Psychologists like Mary Ainsworth and Elizabeth Meins had written prolifically about the importance of the bond between the primary caregiver and infant. Meins reported that mothers who took the time to attribute meaning to their infant's early vocalizations were more likely to have toddlers who were securely attached. She described this approach as "mind-mindedness." And of course, I wanted a securely attached toddler (!)

In fact, Meins called out how another researcher had described that "Understanding why sensitive responsiveness contributes to a secure attachment, and how this is associated with later working models of self and relationships, may be the *most important* theoretical problem for [attachment] researchers in years to come."

The "most important theoretical problem" were the words used. I remember thinking deeply about my situation, and knowing that, although I could likely find a caregiver or day-care center that could subscribe to theories like mind-mindedness, I had no guarantee of it, and my income wasn't high enough to be certain that I would find the right one.

At that point, I wasn't willing to risk my offspring's development with someone who might be making a wage that didn't permit him or her to have a decent standard of living and could potentially be unhappy to be caring for my kid. I know this sounds dramatic. But the whole experience of becoming a new mother was dramatic for me as a 27-year-old with a fledgling career, living in a fourth-floor walkup, railroad apartment in New York City. I, like many other women, thought deeply about the role I was taking on, and obsessed about getting it all right, sometimes to my own detriment. And frankly, my body was a mess of stretched skin and fluctuating hormones, so even after three months I didn't feel physically ready, either. So I made the call to my employer to let them know that I wouldn't be coming back, and stared into the eyes of this small human, determined to take this new role seriously. A year and a half later, we went on to have another child, and I continued my responsibilities as a full-time parent for years.

But after some time, as my kids got a bit older, I wavered in my decision to give up my professional pursuits. I knew I wanted to make and contribute more financially. Shortly after the birth of our second child, we had made the move so many make to the suburbs. In our case, we'd also taken on a complete renovation project of a historic house. But my options for workforce reentry were scarce. The gap on my resume looked like just the word sounded—a gap in ambition—not a purposeful plan I had crafted to focus on personalized learning and caregiving in partnership with my husband. My volunteer roles as a library board director, and the skills I'd developed researching, managing, and in some cases implementing renovation projects did little to externally enhance my resume. I quickly realized that any step I took back in would likely be a step back from where I had left off, and would still create logistical challenges.

So I explored other ideas, and I identified some opportunities in the nontech environment I had entered, which contrasted sharply with the high-tech environment in which I had previously worked, and saw an opportunity for a business.

I went on to start a software company, be the CEO, raise capital, provide value to customers, sell the business, lead a division within a billion-dollar company, and be recognized as a "Woman to Watch in Tech" by the *Boston Business Journal* and as a "ChangeMaker" by *HUBWeek*. I became a board director of a private equity–backed company, a managing director at a world-class investment firm, and in addition I think I'm a pretty engaged mom to my now-teenage boys. Although this was not a straightforward or easy path, I don't think it would have been possible if I had stayed on the traditional career path. By starting my own company, I was able to gain a set of experiences that are difficult to get in a siloed organization, and I was able to do it while more fully integrating my work in my life. I made these decisions several years before Sheryl Sandberg's book *Lean In* was published, and a decade later the conversation on women and work has not quieted down.

Moving Past the Binary Set-Up

In early 2019 former U.S. first lady Michelle Obama made a passing comment while on a book tour in New York, simply noting that "lean in" doesn't work all of the time. Her casual remarks unleashed a firestorm of debate. Dozens of media outlets, including *The Guardian*, *Fortune*, *Newsweek*, NBC, and the *Washington Post* all ran with the story. Headlines screamed "Michelle Obama Slams Sheryl Sandberg's Lean In Theory!" "Michelle Obama Believes Lean In Doesn't Work!" It was as if the collective voice of the predominately male-owned media had reared its head to seize hold of any conversation on the topic of women in the workplace to say, "I told you so! You really can't have it all—even Michelle Obama agrees!" And knowing that, as the *New York Times* reported in 2018, 86% of all women become mothers, it was no wonder that the topic quickly added to the national dialogue. But as I read the stories and listened to the ensuing heated discussions that unfolded on whether women could really have it all, I had a different thought. **I thought, "Yes, you can . . . but not like this."**

A Little Background on *Lean In*

Like millions of other people, I read Sheryl Sandberg's 2013 book *Lean In* and was motivated by it to rethink many social norms I had long unconsciously accepted. Her book, which encourages women to double down on their careers and assert their leadership skills, inspired me to continue to move my business, which I had started after stepping away from the traditional corporate world for a few years to be with my young children, forward. In fact, I was so inspired by *Lean In* that I was profiled on the Lean In website as a case on "Taking Risks" in 2013 (https://leanin.org/stories/claudia-reuter). However, I also understand why many argue that leaning in doesn't work. The book has managed to be a part of a national conversation for more than six years, and there are myriad reasons why one could argue that leaning in is unrealistic. Yet, I don't think it's the act of leaning in that doesn't work. It's not the pursuit of meaningful work or the desire to lead, and earn a meaningful wage, that doesn't work. It's the structures into which we're leaning that make it look so difficult and that make it is difficult to lean in.

Many corporate structures are rooted in a past that no longer exists: single-earner, male, and ethnically homogeneous. As Marissa Orr describes in her 2019 book *Lean Out*, "Our systems must evolve, and until they do they're leaving a treasure of diverse talent on the table." One solution Orr offers is to "recognize the limitations of the system in which we work, and understand that it cannot always fulfill our deepest human needs.... When we recognize that we're looking for satisfaction in all the wrong places, the pain of our jobs begins to release its grip, and we can find alternative ways to fulfill our needs." In *Lean Out*, Orr candidly describes her experience of parting ways with Facebook. In her book, she dives into research on whether women even want the leadership roles that Sandberg rallies for women to go after, and offered statistics showing that, in fact, very few women or men want to be CEOs or high-level managers. Instead, she advocates for directing dollars toward supporting women in lesser positions and dropping the focus on getting more women into leadership positions within today's corporate structures.

I understand her point, as well as the media frenzy that followed Michelle Obama's comment. But rather than debate whether women should lean in or lean out, why not offer an alternative, one that empowers women and men to redesign the very structures that are broken and to build the lives they want right now? I do think that many of the challenges Orr describes might be solved with more women in positions of leadership; although it's true that not everyone wants to be the leader, if those who do lead change the systems for others in the process, everyone could benefit greatly.

So Why Not Lean In by Starting Up and Move Past the Binary Setup?

Many women jumped deeply into their careers following the success of *Lean In* and its affiliated groups or circles, of which I'm also a member. Speaking with a number of recent college graduates at a university alumni event earlier this year, I heard first-hand how the impact of *Lean In*'s success, coupled with the current college student-loan crisis, has left many younger women stressed and anxious, wondering how they will blend the careers they've prepared for and the families they may want someday. And the backlash that has erupted against *Lean In* actually reinforces the idea that we are all somehow choosing between "work" and "family," choices that, as Tina Fey famously called out in her book *Bossypants*, men are seldom—if ever—asked to make.

The implication in creating a dialogue on leaning in versus leaning out is that it allows the myth to persist that those are the only two options. The message is an either/or, binary proposition: either we work with what exists today or we step away from our passions or desire to lead. I don't think that was Sandberg's intention when she wrote *Lean In*. In fact, she called out how women should work to adjust the system, and to hold men accountable as partners as they lean in to careers. But by setting up a "lean in versus lean out" dialogue in our society, we are reinforcing a dichotomy in which other options don't really exist. And it's true that for those without an MBA or law degree, or a supportive partner, or the income to support a full-time nanny or childcare provider, there is no real option to lean in to today's corporate environment with any expectation of career progression.

The invitation extended by today's corporate environment, in which only 17% of companies even offer a few weeks of paid maternity leave, let alone provide flexible working environments, is to simply get through it. Office hours seldom align with school hours, forcing parents to work part-time, work after-office hours, or seek childcare. The cost of childcare alone can be as high as university tuition—tens of thousands of dollars per year. The idea of getting through it, that you can (or should) just suffer through a few years of high-cost childcare before the public school system doors open is unacceptable. The idea that the bump in your 401K and potential career advancement will make the long days with paltry take-home pay and sleepless nights easier is also unacceptable. And the idea that the extra effort required to externally appear to make it all look easy is worth it is untenable. I can't think of many people who are motivated and inspired by compound interest or the potential for a promotion alone.

But it's also just as true that you can't comfortably lean out without a supportive partner or the income to support a part-time or single-earner lifestyle. Many people who step away from the workforce are doing so by cobbling together savings and looking for discounts to simply make life feel somewhat comfortable. The structures that are in place make it challenging for people who are primary caregivers to stay in an organization because they were not designed for caregivers. They were designed for people who already have support—child, family, parent. That's why approximately 43% of women leave the traditional workforce at some point in their careers. And even if they do reenter the traditional workforce, they are usually offered positions at lower wages from when they left. That wage and time gap then partially explains why there are fewer women in leadership positions, and why only a small percentage of Fortune 500 companies or corporate board members are women. I think it also helps explain why, in 2019, we still don't see a large percentage of men willing to take on the role of primary caregiver, because even our societal views of caregiving itself are often binary. There is a tendency to view women (and men) who opt out of the traditional workforce to care for children as either wholly unambitious or, conversely, worthy of being put on a pedestal for modeling excellent personalized caregiving and upholding the romantic ideal of motherhood.

Likewise, a recent study from the Pew Institute showed that only 8% of respondents thought that having a father home was beneficial, whereas 76% responded that fathers should be at work.

As Susan Magsamen, executive director of the International Arts and Mind Lab at the Brain Science Institute for Johns Hopkins University, pointed out on my podcast *The 43 Percent* in 2019, "We pay for what we value, and we don't value childcare, we don't value early childhood education, and we don't pay for it. It's what women do." So we have systems in place that encourage us to believe that the option before us is to lean in to a career while tending to the task of parenting quietly and unseen, or to publicly lean out, essentially giving up our claim to the monetary benefits that enhance our well-being in our capitalist society. In both scenarios we acknowledge that caring for children needs to happen, but, as Magsamen pointed out, we don't value it financially. It's worth noting that at various points in this book, I call out how the high price of childcare can consume a large percentage of your take-home pay and factors into the decision to lean in or lean out. The not-so-subtle additional point here, though, is that the "high price" is not often more than your take-home pay. If it were, more people would actually look to become childcare providers to earn a decent living. Instead, childcare is just expensive enough to cause challenges for those not yet earning a six-figure salary, but low-cost enough to be insufficient to provide for a high quality of life for those who pursue it as a profession.

The Privilege of Flexibility at Work

As I reread *Lean In* in 2019, the chapter called "The Myth of Doing It All" caught my attention. In that chapter, Sandberg suggests that, with the advent of technology, employers can shift to "focusing on results [which] would benefit individuals and make companies more efficient and competitive" rather than judging time at the office. The central idea is that many of the constraints that women face are related to time management and the structures that were put into practice without having the whole person in mind. Sandberg recalls a time when she adjusted her schedule to have her first and last meetings of the day at another facility so she could see her child before and after work without other employees noticing. To her point, she wasn't working any less; in fact, she was working more. But in her mind there was a stigma associated with simply appearing to shorten her workday, especially because it was in an effort to see her child.

That stigma is the shadow of the existing corporate walls. By sharing that story of hiding her schedule, Sandberg not only identified one of the main challenges parents, and, in particular, moms, have in the workplace; she also highlighted the privilege she had in making that decision, a privilege that those lower on the career ladder seldom have. It's no wonder her book has become as divisive as it is inspiring.

It was with similar outrage that people responded to stories of Yahoo's first female CEO, Marissa Mayer, setting up a nursery for her new baby in the office. As *The Guardian* pointed out, some were upset that she was taking such little time off, while others were frustrated that she had to talk about it. The lean in or lean out debate is really a critique of how women behave in a workforce that was never designed with them in mind and hasn't put a high financial value on caregiving, despite the relative high cost to families.

I highlight so much backstory on women as mothers (which is not to say that all women will or should become mothers) because 86% of women do become mothers at some point, and they often become mothers just as their careers reach a critical inflection point. Most people with college degrees who follow a traditional career ladder reach the point of management or directorship during their early 30s, approximately 10 years into their careers. This, of course, is also the exact time that many women and men look to start families. According to a recent study from the *New York Times*, while the average age at which a woman has her first child is approximately 26, the average age that a woman with a college education has her first child is now 31. And that age is consistent across the United States, whether she is in Missouri or New York City.

So Let's Explore Another Option: Entrepreneurship

There's an option that empowers women to lean in, not to the systems and corporate structures that others created long ago, but to the new systems we can create today. What if we elevated the conversation by encouraging more women to enter entrepreneurship?

I write this not in an attempt to put more pressure on people or make people feel more frazzled. I can already hear people saying, "But startup life is known to be stressful—now I have to figure out how to manage that as well?" That response is a by-product of trying to work with corporate systems and structures that really haven't been around that long and certainly were not designed with both men and women in mind.

Consider that less than a century ago, when many of the current leaders of Fortune 500 companies, U.S. Senators, and House Representatives, were young adults, employers were still able to discriminate based on gender and pregnancy. Since fighting for and achieving the right to vote in 1920, women have continued to lobby and push against the existing systems, making large and small advancements along the way. But the underlying thread is that we're asking for permission from the existing patriarchal setup.

Consider again that it wasn't until the 1970s that a women could even easily obtain credit without a male co-signer. The implications of this, of course, were that it was incredibly difficult until very recently for a woman to obtain a credit line to attempt to start her own business or to buy property. With that in mind, it's easy to understand how it was also culturally empowering for women to actually remain focused on the path of supportive wife to a successful partner, rather than focusing on career ascension or entrepreneurship.

And while that ability to obtain credit was certainly progress from achieving the right to vote, more than 50 years went by between the two events. According to research from the World Economic Forum, at our current pace, it will take 170 years to achieve gender parity in the workforce. This slow-moving drive to equity is mounted against much of the corporate schedule and formulated workweek we currently take for granted and are simply by-products of the shift to mass production that happened before the advent of modern technology and the internet.

The beauty of a startup is that you create value in the economy and you also control your day. When you start a business, you are *automatically* in a leadership position. You don't need to wait in line, and you get to make the decisions that are best for the company, including structures such as office hours, location, and other policies. You have the freedom to create the business you want and to build the life you want at the same time.

As new startups are formed, they rarely look like traditional companies. They often have flexible schedules, unlimited vacation, bring-your-dog-to-work options, casual dress, and other more modern policies. And although many don't succeed, many startups have disrupted traditional businesses in ways no one could have imagined earlier. Consider that according to a study by "Innosight," which *Harvard Business Review* referenced in a 2017 article, by 2027, 75% of today's Fortune 500 companies will be displaced. So why not start to build a company that could be on that list of disruptors, and create a new set of structures in the process?

I am confident that we can convert the debate into a conversation that promotes more than the either/or choices most people believe they're limited to, by encouraging and supporting women to start up as another alternative. By starting up you can build the life *you* want, with the rules that *work for you*, and this book will show you how. (Exciting, right?)

Win or Lose, How Do I Know You Can Do This?

Because I've done it, and so have countless others. Many people have highlighted that, while Sandberg noted that 43% of women still step away from the workforce when they have children, she offered only one solution for them: just "lean in," while at the same time acknowledging the deep value they provide by stepping away. In 2003, I found myself among those 43% of women Sandberg referenced and took a different path that has enabled me to develop a career I am passionate about while also engaging deeply with my young family.

While I think there is much that can be done within existing corporate structures to make it easier for people, and in particular for women, to bring their whole selves to work, I also think we have a unique opportunity to fix what we don't like about the system by starting up. If more women lean in by starting up, they can change the structures, set the corporate culture that works for them, and by default start to fill the current leadership gender gaps.

I also know that my experiences as a stay-at-home mom have helped me be more, not less, successful in my career. By starting my own company, I didn't sheepishly come in a step or two down the ladder from when I left the workforce, apologizing for the time I took in my one life to focus on my young children. Instead, I jumped back in at the highest rung, as CEO. And when I later joined a large organization with a market cap of more than $1 billion, I did not have any reservations about asserting my leadership skills and knew how to work cross-functionally with others, in part because of my extremely varied experiences as an entrepreneur.

I don't pretend to have all the answers, and I know from experience that the entrepreneurial path is not an easy one. It's challenging, messy, and filled with uncertainty. But it's also incredibly rewarding, and has the potential for personal and professional advancement that other paths don't.

Why This Book Is for *You*

In this book, I'm excited to help you on this path to entrepreneurship by providing the essential steps to take, along with the tools and resources you can use along the way. Wherever you are on your journey—whether you're simply thinking about starting up, or relatively far along—you'll find something to help and will be prepared to change the rules for yourself and others, one entrepreneur at a time.

Moreover, I am confident that we can move beyond topics like "having it all" or "figuring out balance" and instead talk about the things a person can do to take control of her life. *Lean In* ends by asking all of us to continue the conversation on women, work, and the will to lead. My hope with this book is that we do more than keep talking. I am confident that we can tackle the bigger issues that women and men face as they work to build meaningful lives and careers. There are plenty of stories on why being an entrepreneur is hard, and I know many people may be daunted by the idea of taking that path. But there are also many stories that are seldom told of incredibly successful female entrepreneurs that you'll learn more about in this book as well. That's why I'm excited to share what's possible, and help you on your journey to building a business and the life you want.

Are you ready to get started?

I know you can do this. . . .

* * *

How to Read This Book

The book is divided into three sections, each containing multiple chapters, developed to help you build your business:

    I. Get Ready to Start Up
   II. Building for Scale and Avoiding the Traps
  III. Lead and Operationalize

Section I is designed to help articulate the reasons to consider entrepreneurship and the initial steps you'll need to take to get started.

Section II is designed to help entrepreneurs as they work to develop their initial business plans and consider funding.

Section III is designed to help entrepreneurs who have successfully built a business consider how to effectively lead and operationalize.

In each chapter, you'll find a brief narrative that helps to outline the challenges entrepreneurs, and, in particular, women, often face, by leveraging fictional characters, a real-world example from my experiences or other well-documented scenarios, and practical resources that range from tools to create business plans to guided meditation. I've organized the book in a simple, formulaic way so you can read cover to cover, or skip to the chapters that are of most interest to you.

As I set out to write this book, the individual challenges that women encounter along their professional and personal journeys felt too big to take on by simply sharing my own story. That's why each chapter starts with a brief narrative of fictional characters, designed to explore the various challenges that women face as they navigate their careers and consider entrepreneurship.

To help you keep track of who's who, here's a list of the cast of characters.

- **Jill Saunderson:** An experienced executive. Currently serving as a senior executive for a large company, she also serves on several advisory boards. A leader in her tight-knit community, she also actively mentors other women.
- **Maria Paola:** An entrepreneur and software developer. She's building her startup company by night and coding by day at her day job.
- **Sophie Anderson:** A former director of marketing for a large company who is now a stay-at-home mom.
- **Jake Anderson:** Sophie's husband, who is a mid-level manager for a financial services firm.
- **Carolyn Robinson:** A mom and friend of Sophie's.
- **Hannah Smith:** A project manager for a mid-size software company, struggling to find a path to promotion and advancement.
- **Stan Brown:** A project manager for the same mid-size software company that Hannah works for. He's a confident and trusted peer mentor to Hannah in many ways.
- **Allen Monroe:** Hannah and Stan's direct manager. He's a senior leader in the company.

Through the fictional narrative, you'll gain a deeper understanding of the challenges many of the statistics and studies highlight. The second portion of each chapter is designed to pragmatically break down the challenge described and provide practical resources to solve them.

These tools, which range from drafting your first business plan to guided meditation techniques, will empower *you* to build the business and life you want.

So let's get started!

You can do this!

Section I

Get Ready to Start Up

Any time is a good time to start a company.
—*Ron Conway, investor, SV angel*

Chapter 1

So You Want More

Get Off the Fence, Start a Business, and Create the Life You Want

What you'll take away from this chapter:

In this chapter, we'll explore the reasons to start your own company, and why it's never too late or too soon to get started. You'll also find a set of resources designed to help you track some of the most basic things you'll need if you decide to get started.

The Monthly Mentor Gathering

Hannah pulled into the driveway, which was already packed with the other guests' cars, and double-checked herself in the rearview mirror before stepping out to walk up to the front door. Jill Saunderson had offered to host the monthly social club for women in the community, and everyone was buzzing about it. Jill was known to be incredibly accomplished, and Hannah recalled how flattered she had been to receive an invitation to the gathering. Hannah smiled as she saw the care that Jill had put into the event. Paper luminary candles lined the walkway, creating a festive atmosphere for the evening ahead. This was just the kind of detail that Hannah admired, but rarely implemented. Hannah had moved to Fisher's Landing a year earlier and was still getting used to the organized social activities of the tight-knit community. As Hannah reached to press the buzzer, Jill swung open the front door, revealing the warmly lit foyer. "Oh fantastic, you're here!" Jill had a way of making everyone feel welcome. "We've been waiting for you! Let me take your coat, and go make yourself comfortable in the living room."

Hannah unbuttoned her jacket and passed it to Jill before scanning the room to her right. The gas fireplace was on, lighting the room softly. Wine glasses and water tumblers were strategically placed on the coffee table, along with platters of cheese and crackers. About 10 other women were sitting comfortably and chatting. Many of them looked up, smiling warmly, as Jill announced Hannah's arrival. Sophie, a stay-at-home mom, patted the open spot next to hers on the plush sofa and called out quickly, "Hannah, come sit over here, I've been dying to catch up." Hannah had met Sophie a few times at other events, and felt relieved to see her.

"How's everything going? Job okay?" It never felt like niceties when Sophie started her questions. She always seemed genuinely interested, which made it easy to quickly open up.

"Yeah, everything's great," Hannah said. "I just got a good review at work—but I have to admit, I feel like I'm not rising fast enough."

"Good reviews are wonderful, but I'm sure you were ready for a promotion, right?" Sophie asked. "You've been there for what, four years now?"

"Yeah—that's basically it. I just thought that for sure this would be the year, and I know I shouldn't be annoyed, but I was when I saw that Stan got a title bump and I didn't." Hannah took a deep breath as she recalled hearing the news about Stan.

Sophie rolled her eyes and said, "Ugh, that's so frustrating. I remember those days. I'm loving life right now with the kids, and part of me can't imagine going back to the corporate world, but believe me, sometimes I wish I could."

"The grass is always greener, right?" Hannah said this, but actually questioned a little what she meant by it.

Hannah reached over to pour a glass of water, and Maria squeezed in between them. "Hi, ladies! I couldn't help but overhear the conversation. Have either of you ever thought about just starting your own company?"

"Sure, a few times, but I just don't see how I could make it work." Sophie was already thinking of childcare challenges and the relatively lean bank account in her home.

Hannah nodded. "I don't have the childcare pressures that Sophie has, but I don't think I'm far enough along in my career for anyone to take me seriously as an entrepreneur. I'm not even sure what I would do."

Jill, who had been making her way around the room, made her way into the conversation as well. "Maria—I'm sure we're all capable of doing it, but it seems like such an exhausting uphill battle, doesn't it? Even if I had a fabulous new business idea, I'm pretty sure no one would fund any of us. I mean, I read the other day that of all companies that try to get funding, only 2% do, and of those 2% only 2% are led by women."

Hannah and Sophie nodded in unison. "Exactly, 2% of the 2%."

"But guess what? I'm starting a business right now," Maria said. "I recognized where there was a huge gap in the customer experience service market, and I'm working on a SaaS solution that I think is really going to transform businesses."

"What? That's so ambitious of you, Maria," Hannah said. "I had no idea you were working on that." Hannah thought about all the times that her customer experience software at work had frustrated customers and employees.

"Wow. I couldn't help but overhear that one! A software company. Maria—I'm impressed." Carolyn turned around abruptly from another conversation and casually leaned over the back edge of the sofa.

Maria looked up, smiling, getting animated. "Yes, I started by spending just a few hours a week on it. And I'm obviously being careful not to use my company's equipment, and double-checked with corporate to make sure they didn't have a problem with it. But now I'm dedicating many of my off hours to getting things off the ground. My plan is to get a prototype completed, and then test it out in the market. I'm not going to quit my day job until I've validated it, but I really think I'm on to something.... And, I feel like those numbers you were talking about (the 2%!) would change if even more of us got started. Sophie, you could figure out the life that works for you and your family. Hannah, you could stop worrying about your next promotion and start building something that mattered to you. Carolyn, if I recall, you've always got a ton of ideas and could put them to use. Jill, you've been pro-moted a million times in the last few years and are considered a rock star at your company. Why not put that energy into your own business?"

"I don't know. I guess I just didn't think I could . . ."

* * *

Real-World Experiences and Opportunities

Does this conversation sound familiar to you? Have you thought about starting your own business, but struggled to make it a reality because you thought the odds were stacked against you, or you simply didn't know where to get started?

Do you have a burning desire to build a solution that could transform businesses, communities, or the lives of ordinary people, but you're not quite sure how you would get it off the ground? If, like Hannah, Sophie, Carolyn, or Jill, you've thought about starting a business, but worried that you couldn't do it, this book will show you that "yes, you can." With the right skills, mindset, fortitude, confidence, and support, you can start and build a business, and create the life you want. And what's just as exciting is the potential this has for everyone.

If you're like Maria, and you've already started working on a game-changing solution, this book will help you on the next steps in your journey. If, like Hannah, you're at the very beginning of your career, and are just ready to explore entrepreneurship, you'll discover all the options you have before you now. And, as Maria pointed out, as more women start their own businesses, more women will fill the gender gap in leadership, which in turn will create more opportunities for leaders to empower and invest in more women.

Entrepreneurship as the Path Forward

The statistics that the characters were tossing around in the previous section are getting slightly better, but leave much to be desired. Here are some things to consider:

- More than 70% of high school valedictorians are females and more than 50% of college graduates are women, yet only 5% of Fortune 500 CEOs are.

- While women in the United States are starting businesses at higher rates than ever, of all venture capital (a form of financing provided by firms to small, early-stage, emerging companies with high growth potential) in 2019, only 2.2% went to women. This is up a percentage point from 10 years earlier, but still represents just a very small piece of the venture pie.
- Only 17% of corporate board seats are held by women.
- Women are 21% more likely to be considered top performers in corporations, but those under the age of 40 are less likely to receive a promotion than men.
- 43% of women continue to leave the workforce when they have children and 85% of women become mothers.
- Only 17% of U.S. companies offer paid maternity leave, and even fewer offer any type of paternity leave.

These statistics certainly seem to reinforce the challenges that Hannah, Sophie, and Jill discussed. As Jill described, knowing that only a very small percentage of funding goes to women, why even bother trying? And with only 17% of U.S. companies offering paid maternity leave, which I think is just one component of benefits that parents need, it's not hard to understand why 43% of women step away from careers as they start families. So why is Maria's idea of entrepreneurship one to consider?

Someone who starts their own business immediately steps into a leadership position. And when you're in charge, you get to set your own hours, create your own rules, and build the business that is right for you. If you're excelling at work, have amazing ideas, but are not getting the promotion you want, **you can** start your own business and go sell a solution back to your old boss. This book will also teach you to develop the skills that will get you that promotion, and help you as you work to make bigger asks down the road.

If you find yourself among the 43% who left the workforce to lead at home and care for others, **you can** step back in through entrepreneurship. If you're already in a leadership position, but you have a creative urge to build something with more ownership and impact, **you can** put those skills you use to deliver for everyone else into your own business. Moreover, you won't be alone.

Women are starting businesses at an unprecedented rate, and the mainstream media is just starting to take note.

According to a 2018 study by American Express, the number of women-owned businesses increased by 3,000% since 1972. Such exponential growth is obviously related to the fact that prior to 1978 women couldn't get lines of credit without a male co-signer, and naturally that change has impacted the number of women who have been able to get started. But it also highlights the drive that women have to lead and operationalize.

What's Holding You Back?

If you picked up this book, you may be interested in starting your own business today, or you may simply be frustrated with the options you believe are available to build the life you want. Wherever you are on your journey, statistics like those mentioned earlier often do more to reinforce ideas of what's possible (or not possible).

We have had no shortage of images of studious young women in books and media. (Think Anne Shirley from *Anne of Green Gables*, Hermione from *Harry Potter*). But how many strong, female CEOs can you think of? While a few actual CEOs may have popped into your head, like Meg Whitman of HP or Mary Barra of General Motors, it's much easier to rattle off the names of hundreds of men, and it's not easy to think of fictional female CEOs. And if someone were to ask you to think of what a startup CEO looks like, what would come to mind? Many people still think of a young guy in a hoodie as a startup CEO and a middle-aged guy in a Patagonia vest as his investor. While studies that uncover the statistics on women in leadership are important, they can also serve to make women feel even more certain that the odds are stacked against them. But I'm also excited to highlight in this book some of the stories of women who have become CEOs. While seldom discussed, and rarely highlighted in texts on innovation or business, there are examples of women who have done it, and you'll learn more about some of them throughout this book.

The reasons women are not achieving certain career milestones or stepping out of the workforce are conditioned, learned, and systematized. In a consumer society, where marketing is thrust on all of us from an early age, believe it or not, we're regularly confronted with imagery of people in different roles, based on what that company is trying to peddle. We're brought up seeing images of the mom in the nice kitchen, or the character on a TV show acquiescing to the male boss, or the words repeated over to us like, "just be nice." That's societal conditioning.

We learn things through reward systems. So if we continue to reward girls for being submissive, polite, and coloring within the lines, and we reward boys for being adventurous, we will continue to see people taking actions that reinforce those traits. It's not that girls are less adventurous, or have any less of a natural desire to lead, but they are often rewarded for exhibiting different behaviors—and we typically see more of what we reinforce with rewards.

So the statistics are daunting, and we've set up a society that does actually encourage women to step down from jobs following childbirth. With fewer than 17% of U.S. companies offering paid maternity leave, and childcare costs that can be as high as university fees, there is literally no reward for staying on a professional career journey. Rather, we've created a motherhood penalty. Many parents are left to piece together some vacation days and sick days to simply be able to take a maternity leave, and then watch in dismay as a large percentage of their take-home pay goes to cover daycare costs once they go back to work.

The systems that exist today were designed for and by men and, moreover, for men with women behind the scenes supporting them, and as women have made advances in the workforce, they've often done so by figuring out how to fit into those systems and constructs.

It's no wonder that we often see women who are in leadership positions working to fit into the environments that hold so many men in positions of power by setting their personal lives and stories aside. For example, when you see candidates running for office, we often see pantsuits and shoulder pads. The image shared through visual rhetoric is that in order to succeed in leadership you need to dress like a man, which of course implies that the role was actually designed for men. That's systematized. And that's just one of the subconscious patterns I'm hoping to help break down with this book.

If you picked up this book, you are likely considering what your next steps may look like. You may be ready to jump in and get started, or you may be at the early stages of exploration and not feel ready. Wherever you are on our journey, you will find resources in the book to help. **You can do this!**

My Journey to Becoming a Startup Entrepreneur

As I am writing this, I have what most people consider a dream job. I work as a managing director at Techstars, the worldwide network designed to help entrepreneurs succeed. I get to invest money into companies working on game-changing emerging technologies and help those companies scale as they participate in Techstars' highly regarded accelerator program. If you take a peek at my LinkedIn profile, you'll see some titles that reflect what my friends and I call my "big kid jobs" (Senior Vice President, Head of Labs, CEO for Venture Backed Startup, Board Director, etc.), along with some industry awards like "BBJ Women to Watch in Tech" and "HubWeek ChangeMaker"). But if you look more closely, you'll notice something else: There's a three-year gap between my tech job at an investment bank and my position as CEO.

Guess what I was doing in that time? I was leaning out. I had a baby, who's now 16, then another one, who's now 14, and as a result of many of the statistics I cited earlier in this chapter, I stepped out of the workforce. I'm by no means advocating that women step out of the workforce, but I think it's important to note that I was passionate about my career and still couldn't figure out how to integrate it with my changed family life. At the end of the day, I wanted to be with my young children more and didn't see any ways to give my best to my job at the same time. So how did I get to a point where I was running digital services and a labs innovation team with a multimillion-dollar budget to manage existing services and build new products for a billion-dollar company?

I started up.

What Starting Up as a Stay-at-Home Mom Looked Like

By the time my boys were toddlers, I knew I needed to make an additional income for my family at some point, and I had researched a number of options with my husband's support. Believe it or not, starting my own business actually looked more promising than trying to explain my gap years to a new potential employer. Starting a business was also a way to continue to own my daily routine, and allowed me the flexibility I wanted to spend my day with my children. I could work on contracts and negotiations during their naptimes and stay up late into the evenings working on the business. But during the day, I could also manage to focus my attention on these little humans I truly enjoyed. Of course, that didn't come without challenges as I later sought to raise investment capital to grow the business.

In 2010, as I was searching for investment, I found myself sitting on the floor of my older son's closet, surrounded by Legos, a Buzz Lightyear action figure, and a flock of dust bunnies, waiting for a conference call to begin. I had in front of me what so many entrepreneurs hope for, an unsigned term sheet from investors that outlined their offer to provide a few hundred thousand dollars in capital in exchange for equity, or ownership, in my business.

As I picked the lint off my yoga pants, I silently prayed that my young boys would not start screaming in the middle of the call. I wanted to impress the men on the other end of the line—a senior executive advisor, my lawyer, and the two investors who had provided the term sheet. While I hoped the investors would ultimately invest in my fledgling software company, which I had built to help educators manage accreditation and assessment processes, my mentor and lawyer cautioned me that the term sheet was filled with some language that they felt was overreaching. If I recall correctly, one of them even used the term piggish to explain it to me.

While I knew I was off to strong start because I had a few key sales and had just completed nine months of negotiation with a national nonprofit organization, I was also an unproven entrepreneur, lacking an Ivy League degree, living far away from Silicon Valley or any tech hub at the time. But I needed capital to grow the business, and this was the only term sheet I had, so I was ready and excited to negotiate. I remember waiting for these people I hoped to impress to join the call, and imagining what their experiences were like. In contrast to my own surroundings, I was sure my lawyer was in a slick boardroom with his administrative assistant just the snap of a fingeraway, and the senior executive was probably in a corner office, while the investors were likely riding in the back of a luxury car, fielding numerous requests from other entrepreneurs like me.

As they each joined the call, and we got past the customary greetings, one of the investors cut to the chase. "We're going to slow this down. We want to get some other investors involved." This, of course, brought the conversation to an abrupt ending. *Forget negotiating the terms—they weren't even prepared to sign their own term sheet yet.* Within seconds, all of the men jumped off the line, and I sat there on the floor, stunned at the turn of events. But just as I leaned my head on the wall, ready to take a moment to feel the frustration, I heard the scream I had worked hard to avoid: "*Mommy*—where are you?"

I jumped to my feet and stood for a moment, trying to process what had just happened before running downstairs. I could either forget trying to raise capital or find some new investors. Since I couldn't afford to get additional childcare support at that point, things did not look so great.

But I went on from that day to find the investors I needed, used the capital to continue to develop the business, and we were eventually acquired by another company. From there, I went on to lead digital services and an innovation team at a large corporation, managing a multimillion-dollar budget within a multibillion-dollar company, joined the board of directors for a private equity–backed startup, and am now, as I mentioned, a managing director at Techstars. On paper, my resume looks like a clear progression. In reality, it was anything but that.

You see, after the birth of my first child in 2003, I did what 43% of highly qualified women do: I dropped out of the traditional workforce. That three-year gap on my resume started when I left my promising career as a senior support analyst in the E-comm division of UBS, an investment bank. I had jumped into technology in the late 1990s when companies were eager for anyone who knew HTML, and I had leveraged my liberal arts education to learn new skills in web development and systems administration.

My impression had been that there were few women in banking at that point, let alone women in tech in banking. I recall that during my pregnancy, the bank was making efforts to be more inclusive of women, adding a nursing room to the women's bathroom, and there were some female executives who I considered mentors at the time who offered support. But once I had my first son, I couldn't figure out how I was going to make it work. During my maternity leave, my direct manager left so I had a new boss to impress. The childcare options I found were going to add an hour to my commute and eat up a large percentage of my take-home salary. On top of it all, as one of the first of my friends to have a baby at 27 years old, I was totally unprepared for the state of my hormones, my stretched, sagging body, and the desperation of sleep deprivation.

To put it simply, I was a mess. I had gained 52 pounds during my pregnancy, which seemed impossible, because I threw up nearly every day. Although I had planned to have a natural childbirth, my labor was induced, and I ended up dealing with a massive episiotomy. I literally had to carry an inflatable plastic donut with me for about three weeks because the stitches made it painful to sit down. I also thought I would breastfeed, but realized within the first few weeks that my body wasn't going to cooperate. As my 12 weeks of maternity leave, which statistically I was extremely lucky to have, were coming to an end, I realized I was just starting to lose weight, my baby was just beginning to really smile at me and sleep for more than an hour or two at time, my plastic donut was finally in the trash, and I was just about able to walk up the stairs in my rented fourth-floor apartment in New York City without discomfort. Things were just getting under control, and the idea of starting a new routine, and leaving this baby at daycare that I would have to pay for, just felt completely overwhelming. So that was it. With my partner's support, I quit. And I felt like I had jumped off the deep end of the pool and didn't know how to swim. I swam in that pool of full-time parenting for many years, and with each year, although I was happy to be with my children, I also grew less confident in my ability to jump back into the business sector again.

What I realize now, many years later, is that I wasn't alone. 43% of women step out of the workforce at some point and countless people have experiences that make it challenging to work within today's current business structures. You may be struggling with childcare issues, caring for elders, or simply be dissatisfied with the way business is currently done. None of these challenges means you can't forge a new path. My journey back in to a fulfilling career was possible by creating a startup. At the time I started in 2006, of all companies that went for venture capital funding, only 2% were successful at fundraising, and of them, only 1% (of the 2%) were founded and run by women. If I was able to create a startup as a non-MBA, living in the suburbs, fielding conference calls from a child's closet, *so can you.* While my journey is unique in many ways, I'm confident the challenges I encountered are common, and I'm hopeful that my hard-earned experiences (which include success and failure) will help make things easier for you.

A Manifesto for Women to Become Entrepreneurs, and a Playbook to Help

If you picked up this book, I imagine there is something compelling you to move forward personally and professionally, and something else that you can't quite put your finger on, that might be holding you back. In *Yes, You Can Do This!*, you'll learn all the soft and hard skills needed to start up and scale your business, and create the life you want. This book is as much a manifesto designed to encourage women (and men) to start new companies as it is a how-to-guide for those who are ready to take the plunge. You'll discover the secrets I wish I had had access to earlier in my journey, and will feel empowered to get started.

This book is designed to serve as a playbook for you, as you work to build your business. You can read cover to cover, or skip to the chapters that provide answers to your immediate questions. In each chapter, you'll learn specific skills like developing a financial projections sheet, getting access to full resources, and uncovering the soft skills you can incorporate into your processes to enhance your thinking and management experience.

And I know with the right resources, perspective, and shared experiences, *you can* build the business and life you want.

You can do this!

A Startup Checklist

Table 1.1 provides a very basic view of many of the initial steps you'll need to be aware of as you get started.

Table 1.1   A Basic Business Checklist

Getting Started

Define your purpose.	Write down why your business should exist. What service are you providing? What problem are you solving?
Do a competitive analysis.	Research the competitive landscape. Make a matrix of other companies out there with similar solutions, and see where you think you fit in or compete. Don't limit yourself to companies working directly on your product idea. Look at the broader landscape as well.
Know your customer.	Really research the market to understand who your potential customers are.
Name of company (trademark).	Visit the U.S. Patent and Trademark site (USPTO.gov) to apply for a trademark on your company's name.
Consider your current employer.	If you are still working for another company, be sure to use only your own equipment on your personal time. Also double-check with your corporate counsel to ensure that what you are working on isn't considered a conflict. You want to be fair to your current employer and also ensure that your current company doesn't claim ownership of your work later.
Set up a Tax EIN number (register your business).	Visit the IRS site (https://www.irs.gov/businesses/small-businesses-self-employed/apply-for-an-employer-identification-number-ein-online).
Check your state websites to ensure that you file your business correctly.	Each state has different requirements when starting a business. Even if you incorporate in a state like Delaware, you'll still need to check your state website to make sure you're paying any appropriate fees.
Investigate building a website. Secure a domain name.	Modern sites like wix.com and squarespace.com make it easy for people with no development skills to create a website.
Track your expenses.	You can use tools ranging from Excel to Quickbooks. (You'll likely share these with an accountant later for taxes, so the sooner you start tracking these, the easier it will be.)
If you're starting with a friend, consider creating an operating agreement.	Draft a simple document that outlines the roles of each person in the company, and who owns what percentage of the company. This is an internal document that will help you avoid confusion later.
Create an executive summary, including financial projections and go-to-market plan.	We'll cover this in Section II of this book.

(continued)

Table 1.1 (*Continued*)

Getting Started

Determine if you have any IP on the product you are creating.	If you're developing a unique, innovative product, consider researching whether it is patentable. First visit the USPTO.gov site. Then, if necessary, find a good patent attorney.
Know about sales and use tax.	Again, make sure you visit your local websites, and consult with an accountant once you start buying and selling things to make sure you are handling taxes correctly.
Bootstrap as you can, but be aware of all of your funding choices.	We'll cover this in Section II of this book, but you will want to become aware of all the funding options you have if you need funding.
	This includes local grants, crowdfunding, venture investment, and business loans.

Chapter 2

Reasons to Lead

All the Cool Things You Can Do When You're in Charge

What you'll take away from this chapter:

In this chapter, we'll explore the ways in which starting your own business can actually help you have more flexibility and empower you to rethink the corporate structures that make personal and professional development difficult for so many.

A Little More About Sophie ...

Sophie went home from the social event, thinking deeply about her conversation with Hannah and Maria. The lights were dimmed in her house, and she snuck in the front door quietly, careful not to wake the kids. Jake, her husband of 15 years who she started dating in college, was dozing on the couch with the TV on.

When Sophie and Jake had realized the steep price of childcare, they had essentially flipped a coin to determine who would stay home with the kids for the first few years. At that point in time, they were both relatively early in their careers and earning similar salaries. Jake was in many ways the ideal partner Sheryl Sandberg described in her groundbreaking book *Lean In*. He was always up for splitting household chores, and saw the value in providing high-quality personalized childcare to their own children. As he progressed in his own career while Sophie was with the kids, he regularly acknowledged that he had an easier time rising professionally because he knew Sophie was home with the kids. They had no logistics issues that could interfere with his ability to be present at work. But now that the kids were getting older, he sometimes felt badly that Sophie wasn't getting the same type of recognition he was at his job.

Jake roused himself when Sophie entered.

"Hey, welcome home … You have a good time?"

"Yeah, it was great to catch up with everyone. Kids go to sleep okay?" Sophie squeezed her way into the couch.

"Yeah—there was a bit of arguing, but they're pretty much out," Jake answered with a yawn. Sophie exhaled, reminding herself how lucky she was to have a supportive partner, and felt relieved that the kids were sleeping okay. This was everything she had wanted: a nice home, a solid partner, healthy kids. But she couldn't shake the conversation she had had with Maria, Hannah, and Jill.

"Jake—do you ever wish I was earning more?"

"Soph—we've been over this at least 100 times. Your extra income would be great … but it would fly right out the window to daycare, housecleaners, etc."

"I know, but I would also be contributing to my 401K, which, remember, I'm losing the ability to get compound interest on right now."

"Remember we decided not to worry about that right now?" Jake wondered what had triggered this conversation.

"I know … It's just that tonight, we were all chatting and Maria's doing this whole startup business, Jill's this amazing executive who just got another promotion, Hannah was complaining a little about getting passed over for one, and I just started feeling like I wasn't even in the game."

"You know I think you're central to our family's well-being. I support whatever you want to do, but your old job would crush us right now. With travel, meetings at 6, overnights at conferences … I don't miss any of that." Jake also thought for a moment about how it would make it harder for him to continue to excel at work, but quickly brushed the thought aside, realizing it seemed selfish.

"Me neither. But I do miss adding value in other ways, and being in the game, making a difference out there."

"You're adding tons of value right here." Jake was being sincere in this comment.

"I know, but now that the kids are ready for school, I feel like I could do more during the day— but no normal job would ever have me after taking all of this time off."

"What if I started my own company?" ... Sophie let the words hang a bit as she thought more about what that could look like.

* * *

Why a Business Can Give You the Life You Want

Is this a conversation you've ever had with a spouse or partner? Perhaps, like Sophie, you've taken some time away from the traditional workforce because the structure of your existing role didn't allow you to easily manage your family life.

There is a great deal of dialogue out there on how to reenter the workforce. Over the years, I've seen countless posts on how to explain away your gap years, and on how to be okay with coming back in at a lower level. And in my professional experience, I've encountered many other women who have stepped away from the workforce, and then lost confidence as they worked to step back in. Many struggle to find a new job or take a significant pay cut from their previous salary upon their return. I've never understood why this is the conversation. If someone steps away to add value at home, that doesn't mean they've taken a long vacation; it means they've managed a very different set of projects and situations with no compensation.

I do think more can be done to help women (and men) see the transferable skills they likely developed as a full-time parent, and certainly more can be done to help corporations recognize the value returning parents can have to an organization. See Chapter 11 for more details on the specific ways in which your experiences as a parent could actually make you a better manager. But I also think we have an opportunity to help more women (and men) see that they have other options.

You Can Change the Rules

Starting a business actually gives you more flexibility to change the rules that make balancing a life with work challenging in the first place. Whether you plan on having a family or not, it's important to realize that starting a business lets you define the rules that are right for you and you could make things easier for others in the process. I've used the example of Sophie balancing work and family, because her situation is one of the more complicated balancing acts that can inhibit long-term career progress. To get started, let's take a look at Table 2.1, which shows some of the existing rules we take for granted in society:

Just at a glance you can see that how early you are in your career greatly impacts decisions that you make regarding family. While finances are one factor in decision-making, others are commute time and logistics.

Sometimes the most effective leaders in organizations stay a few minutes (or hours) late to resolve an issue or work to hit a deadline, and doing so in the office can be important optically. But those extra minutes (or hours) can mean the difference between making it to pick children up on time or not.

Likewise, if you're looking to make an impact and lead, there are certainly many paths to do that in companies, but depending on the corporate culture, rising through the ranks may be a long

Table 2.1   The Current " Rules"

The Current Structure	
Normal business hours (40 hours plus commute time)	(+/−1) 8 a.m.–5 p.m. (+/−1) (plus potential travel and other meetings)
Normal school hours	8 a.m.–2:30 p.m. (September–June only)
Average commute time	Nationwide: 26 minutes (in metro areas, more than 30 minutes each way)
Average starting salary for college grads	$40,000
Average college loans	$37,000
Average time for promotion	Two to three years
Average annual salary raise	3% (if promoted, 5–10%)
Average vacation time	Starting two weeks (longer tenure or higher positions may get more than six weeks)
Average cost of nanny	$34,000 per year
Average cost of full-time daycare	$12,000–$18,000 per year
Average cost of weekly housekeeper	$150 per week ($7,800 per year)
Paid maternity or paternity leave	Less than 17% of companies provide it.
Maternity leave usually fesired	Minimum 12 weeks

haul with limited additional income per year. But if you're ready to try your hand at controlling your destiny, and are ready to lead today, why not consider creating your own business?

Startups have consistently led innovations in industry, as well as in how companies function and treat employees. The following is a quick view of some of the changes that startups have made over the years.

Startup Perks That Are Starting to Become More Mainstream

- Unlimited vacation
- Dog-friendly
- Remote work (work from home)
- Free food
- Flexible hours
- Casual dress codes
- Paternity leave
- Massages
- Gym/wellness benefits

When starting your own business, you have the power to change the very structures that confine your decision-making. The following is a list of just some of the rules you could change if you were in charge.

When You're in Charge, You Can:

- Create your own office hours
- Choose whether you work remotely or in an office
- Decide where and what your office is
- Decide whether you'll permit pets at work
- Choose the dress code
- Decide whether you will offer maternity/paternity leave
- Allow people to bring their "whole" self to work
- Determine the types of benefits you'll provide, including childcare components

This list could go on and on. My point is not to dictate what benefits or modifications to typical structures you should create when starting your own business. My point is to emphasize that when you make the decision to create your own business, you are taking a step to create more control over your destiny, and with that comes the ability to create the structures that work for you. Many of the structures we accept as norms in our corporations today have not been around very long in the grand scheme of history. While it's certainly the prerogative of each person to determine the type of structures she will create, I know there is an opportunity to rethink substantial ways in which we work and live.

The History on This Is Still Recent

Consider for a moment that in 1910, only 10% of U.S. citizens graduated from high school, and women could not vote. In 1942, it was completely acceptable to post an advertisement that specified the gender of the applicant. And in 1975, the year in which I was born, women still required spousal approval to open a credit card account. While the Civil Rights Act of 1964 prohibited employers from discriminating based on gender, it wasn't until 1978 that the Pregnancy Discrimination Act was passed to amend it to prohibit employers from discriminating against women who were or planned to become pregnant.

Think about it. For more than 10 years after people agreed that employers shouldn't be able to discriminate based on sex, employers still had a legal way to block the hire of a woman because she might be pregnant or was even considering getting pregnant.

Legislation Can't Be the Only Path Forward

The point here is that many of the conditions to which we are seeking alignment have not really been around that long. But when we work to change them through the traditional system (i.e., legislation), change can be a very long time in coming. While women achieved the right to vote in 1920, more than 50 years passed before some of these other changes took hold. We now look at the daunting statistics on the lack of women in leadership positions and wonder how to resolve it. According to research from the World Economic Forum, at the current rate of change, it will take 170 years to achieve gender parity. In other words, at the current rate of change, we won't see equity in my lifetime or my children's lifetimes. All of these challenges, though, are simply by-products of the first Industrial Revolution and its shift to a factory schedule, which preceded the internet and advances in communication we have today. So why do we continue to align to them, and why should we be willing to wait for things to change?

Books like Tim Ferriss's *The 4 Hour Workweek* have stayed on the *New York Times* best-seller list for years, because people are looking for ways to escape the 9-to-5 grind. It's a factory mindset, after all. Meanwhile, books like Sandberg's *Lean In* or Lois Frankel's *Nice Girls Don't Get the Corner Office* call for women to double down on their careers, buying into the very structures that others (mainly men) are already working to disrupt. What's more, the very advice to lean in to careershas created a "lean in or lean out" debate among many women. All of this seems to enforce a scarcity mindset that says there are not enough slots or enough prosperity for all of us. I think that while we're debating how to conform to the existing constructs, others will completely reboot the system with new advances and potentially leave us the scraps of however the new regime is designed. But Sandberg's point is correct that we need not just step away from any career aspirations because the structures that are in place are challenging.

When I made a decision to start a company, I set my own hours. I worked on my website while my kids were napping. I brought them with me to the bank where I opened my first business account. I drafted my first business plan in the wee hours of the night when my second child would wake up and I couldn't go back to sleep until I was confident he was asleep. While I remember feeling like I had to hide my personal situation from customers, I never hid my business from my family. They were aware at very young ages of the work I was doing, and they were part of it. Even now, all these years later, as I've developed a podcast project and am writing this book, my kids are aware and engaged. My older son helped me figure out the best way of soundproofing to record my interviews, and my younger son will often do his homework at the same time I'm working on my book. He doesn't seem to mind when I toss an idea at him to elicit his feedback.

While I can hyper focus on work and personal activities, I don't feel the need to compartmentalize them. Work is woven into my personal experiences in ways that provide additional opportunities for us to engage with each other, and I hope to provide my children with learning experiences they may not have had traditionally.

For example, I've walked them conceptually through various contracts I've worked on over the years to hear their thoughts on the fairness of certain revenue-share models, and, believe it or not, their gut responses are often just as helpful to me as I think things through as they may be to them to learn. When I've had to attend conferences, I've often tried to have them join me, if not at the actual event, then at least on the trip, so they experience the travel and understand what I am doing when I'm away from them on other occasions.

The earliest parts of a business are not typically in a traditional corporate office. In fact, the startup culture embraces the idea of the company created in a garage. Why not in a living room? Most early company development is focused on research, on product development, initial customer acquisition, and fundraising—all activities that take similar amounts of time that people might spend on things like surfing Instagram or digging into Facebook. In hindsight, I spent a significant amount of time with no pay working to build a business. But I was able to do it with the kids and when the company was in a position to grow, I felt like my kids were growing with it. I recently interviewed author Laura Vanderkam for my podcast, and her perspective on time management is one I unknowingly leveraged years earlier, and one that all of us would be well-served to consider as we work to achieve or do more. Laura has pointed out that we focus on the idea of the 40-hour workweek, as if there are only 40 set hours in which to accomplish professional activities. The remainder of our time must surely go to leisure activities or sleeping. But as Laura describes in her book *168 Hours: You Have More Time Than You Think*, there are actually 168 hours in a 7-day week, and assuming you sleep for 8 hours a night, that leaves you with 112 hours to do with whatever you'd like. Even if you are still working at a traditional 40-hour-week day job, you still have 72 hours per week to accomplish things apart from work or sleep. If you're focused and conscientious with your own time, you actually have much more than you think, whether you are currently a stay-at-home mom or a professional working a 40-hour workweek. You not only have time to start a business, you have an opportunity to rethink how you'll use your time in your new business!

So rather than select an option based on "opt-in" or "opt-out," I think women have a real opportunity to rethink the systems among which we are choosing and hone our leadership skills to create our own businesses that work for us. But before we dig into that, let's go back to the basics. In Chapter 1, you saw a list of high-level items you need to track if you are ready to start a business. As you start to think through the problem you may be solving or the services you may want to deliver, it's helpful to be aware of the different types of businesses you can create.

Table 2.2 shows a short view of them.

Table 2.2   Types of Businesses You Can Start, and Why

Types of Businesses	Basic Needs to Start	Typical Path to Generate Income	Why to Consider This Type
Consulting service	A specialized core service offering (engineering, design, accounting, etc.) Online Web presence	Hourly or project based Local outreach, referral	You have a certain skill or specialization that allows you to set a project-based or hourly rate (business consulting, software development consulting, freelance writing, etc.)
Brick and mortar bsiness (restaurant, retail, laundry, etc.)	Capital sufficient to lease space, hire Legal/local compliance	Foot-traffic customer acquisition	You are passionate about starting a local business with a fixed location (restaurant, coffee shop, retail store, laundromat, etc.)
Scalable corporation	Providing a legitimate solution in a large market Ability to bootstrap Need to consider fundraising	Customer acquisition	You are interested in solving a problem with a large market opportunity (e.g., a new software solution that you could sell to thousands of similar companies). You believe that what you are building can be disruptive.
Nonprofit	A social/societal goal	Income is in support of the mission	You are interested in building a business with a social good/benefit (e.g., creating an organization that could improve education, support disenfranchised groups).

With each of these businesses, you'll need to ensure that you're complying with local and federal tax laws, and tracking your expenses and revenue.

In this book, we focus most heavily on those looking to start a scalable business; however, if you're ready to start a consulting service, brick-and-mortar business, or nonprofit, you'll still find many of the resources in this book relevant and helpful. With each you will need to figure out how to generate revenue, manage your expenses, and clarify your vision.

Are you ready to dig in and get started?

You can do this!

A Historical Snapshot

A quick fact check: As you consider whether to start your own business, consider a few things. Most of the conveniences we take as standard today did not exist 100 years ago. Moreover, most of the rules in our corporate lives today were built with other times and systems in mind. As you think about starting your own business to build the life you want, don't feel constrained by what exists today.

While things have improved over time, what else could change? What else could you do? This isn't a call to action to jump into part-time work or to re-enter the workforce you might have left. This is a call to action to start a new business to build the life you want. As you do so, you might just find that you redefine what's considered the norm in the process, and help others along the way.

You can see in the following figure that while it took 45 years from the time women obtained the right to vote until the Equal Rights Amendment was passed, it took only two years for someone to start building Uber after the introduction of the iPhone. Restating that, only two years after the iPhone was introduced, a company created a solution that completely disrupted the taxi business, a decades-old industry. Companies not only have the potential to bring new solutions to market, but they can literally change the way in which we live. From travel to shopping to communication, there have been countless solutions that have become mainstream in just a few years.

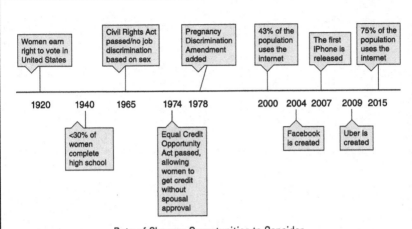

Rate of Change: Opportunities to Consider

So it's worth considering that while technology is accelerating at an exceedingly rapid pace, we have an opportunity to build new businesses to not only personally create the lives we want, but with the potential to disrupt the very challenges we face.

Chapter 3

Stop Believing Your Own Unconscious Bias

Develop the Mindset and Self-Confidence to Be the One in Charge with Gratitude

What you'll take away from this chapter:

In this chapter, we'll explore the ways in which unconscious bias can impact the way in which you behave and the ways in which you are perceived. We'll also explore how expanding your own mindset and developing more self-confidence can help you on your journey.

Hannah at Work

Hannah slipped on her shoes, checked her sweater for lint, and grabbed her computer bag before heading out the door, coffee cup in hand. She had a relatively short commute to work, but used the time to listen to the news and give some additional thought to the day ahead.

She had been working as a project manager for four years for Company X, a mid-sized software company. She was consistently praised for good work by her boss. The projects to which she was assigned were all delivered on time, and with customer satisfaction, but her last review during promotion time had gone the same as the year before. She replayed that conversation in her head as she drove.

"Hannah, I'm thrilled with your work this year. Congratulations, you've received a 4 rating!" Allen, her boss, was about 45 years old, and had been at a few other prestigious companies before joining Company X two years earlier. He rarely made eye contact with her as he spoke, glancing at his computer and phone often.

"Thanks, Allen. I'm thrilled to be working here, and glad the Starship Project went well."

She remembered having felt proud of her accomplishments in that moment, and had gone back to her desk smiling. It was only a few minutes later that Stan had stopped by. A fellow project manager, Stan and Hannah often chatted about projects to which they were assigned and he had also led a strong one this year.

"Hey Hannah—how did review time go?" Stan asked warmly.

"Great! It's nice to know Allen's noticed what I'm doing." Hannah was glad to have a friend in Stan, and was quick to share her accomplishment.

"Awesome, yeah, I was glad they finally promoted some of us project managers." Stan said this assuming both he and Hannah had received promotions because he knew how strong her work had been this year.

Hannah's stomach dropped. "Oh, I didn't get a promotion...."

"Oh, sorry—I just, um, assumed you would have been promoted. I just got a director title and will be taking on a few more teams."

"Oh, wow ... um ... congratulations...." Hannah was doing all the right things, but felt deflated that no one seemed to want to reward her for it.

Later that day, she had gone to the conference room. Many of the chairs were filled so she had sat toward the back ... Stan had confidently grabbed the seat in the center, and smiled as Allen announced his promotion and additional responsibilities. As she drove home, Hannah replayed in her mind how she had sunk more deeply into her chair, her face reddening as she had felt the sting of being overlooked.

With these thoughts in mind, she resolved to go speak with Stan the next day.

She walked through the maze of desks in their open office space and made her way into Stan's office.

"Hey—congrats again on the promotion." Hannah meant it, but had a probing tone to her voice, eager to have a deeper conversation about it.

"Thanks Hannah . . . bummed you didn't get one, but hopefully next year." Stan glanced up from his computer, where he was running budget numbers for the quarter.

Comfortable with Stan as a friend and co-worker, she casually plopped into the chair opposite his desk. "Well, how did you do it? Do you know why Allen gave you a promotion?" Hannah didn't realize how badly she also wanted a promotion until she felt the emotion creep up in her voice as she spoke.

Stan closed his computer, realizing the gravity of the conversation from Hannah's perspective. "Hannah—I asked for one ... a long time ago. I know this company is lucky to have me here crushing it every day. So I set an expectation when I started that I would expect a promotion within two years, assuming, of course, that I delivered." Stan's tone was level and compassionate.

"Oh, I feel kind of silly for saying this, but I guess I figured they would just notice that I was doing a good job, and want to reward me for it." Hannah thought of all the late nights with the team and social events she had skipped to make sure her projects went well.

"Hannah, this isn't school. You need to actually engage in a conversation with your boss. They may not be able to give a promotion, but if that's important to you, you need to let them know so you can plan and manage your own career."

"I hadn't thought about it that way." Hannah stood up, gathering her thoughts as she prepared to restart her day.

Hmm ... Maybe Stan was right—she didn't ask for any of this. In fact, she hadn't thought at all about how she could manage her own career. She was focused on her work, not on managing her career or her boss.

It was later that night, when she went to Jill's social gathering, that she was confronted in another way about personal accountability, self-advocacy, and professional management. Hearing Maria talk about her startup and processing Stan's feedback from earlier in the day left her wondering about what was happening to her versus what she could control.

Making the Ask

The next day, Hannah, saw Allen, her boss, in the hallway near the water cooler.

"Good morning, Hannah."

"Allen, do you have a minute to talk?"

"Of course. Is everything okay?" Allen wasn't an overly concerned manager, but was typically eager to ensure that employees were okay.

"Yes, everything's okay, but I was hoping to talk more about my performance review. Thank you again for the positive feedback and review. I'm glad you know I'm doing a good job managing projects here."

"Well, you earned it. We're glad to have you on board." Allen was being polite, but getting a little impatient.

"I noticed that some of the other project managers at my level were promoted. I'd like to understand what the missing things are that I need to do to be considered for promotion also." Hannah was trying to sound impartial and logical as she spoke, but could tell as she was talking that it was falling flat.

Allen paused for a moment. "I think this is a bigger conversation than one we can have at the water cooler. Let's look for some time and make this a topic this year." Allen thought about how he hadn't fought very hard in the calibration meeting for Hannah's promotion. While he knew she did good work, he assumed she was okay with her current place, and didn't see her as a flight risk. Pushing out the conversation to another time would give him more time to think through his response.

"Oh, okay. Thanks so much." Hannah quickly walked back toward her desk, regretting making the ask at the water cooler, rather than in a formal meeting.

* * *

A Few Things About This Conversation

Do you think Hannah is going to be promoted with this conversation? She may be, but what are some of the unconscious biases that are holding her back?

An unconscious bias is a stereotype that is so ingrained culturally that it becomes automatic and unintentional. Let's take a closer look at what just happened:

1. Notice that Stan did not ask for a promotion. He laid out what he needed from the transactional relationship of doing work. Also, note that he did do the work well. By his and Hannah's statements we know that Stan is a good project manager.
2. Hannah did the same work and is also a good project manager. However, she is expecting to be noticed for her work, rather than advocating for her position.
3. Moreover, Allen, their manager, engaged in the career progression conversation with Stan, but did not think to proactively do so with Hannah, a seemingly strong employee. This may have in part been because she didn't raise the issue. The other side is that in calibration sessions, managers can often only nominate a small percentage of employees for promotion. Hannah's silence may have contributed to Allen's ambivalence, but he was also reacting to Stan's proactiveness.

How We Think and Act Is Conditioned

Certainly, this story has a few stereotypes brewing in it, but the behavior is based on gender studies in education settings. Keep in mind that we tend to develop habits based on attention. We are conditioned to exhibit habits for which we are praised rather than those that are ignored. While in theory negative feedback should create less reinforcement of a behavior, sometimes children will develop behaviors based on negative feedback because they respond to feedback or attention, even when it's negative. So it's worth thinking about how the distribution of feedback between genders in the earlier grades could impact behaviors later in the professional sector.

As highlighted in an article from SUNY on educational psychology, multiple studies have shown that teachers are more likely to praise correct knowledge in boys and compliant behavior in girls, while ignoring compliant behavior in boys and correct knowledge in girls. Further, they are more likely to criticize misbehavior in boys and incorrect knowledge in girls. So boys receive feedback that helps them reinforce their efforts to be correct but receive no reward or feedback for being compliant, and girls receive feedback that reinforces that they should exhibit compliant behavior while receiving negative feedback for incorrect knowledge.

You can start to see how boys are basically conditioned to feel that they are always misbehaving or being noncompliant, so they may just become numb to it. They've been rewarded for getting to the correct knowledge or outcome rather than for any perceived good behavior on the way there. Similarly, these types of reinforcing notions make girls more likely to feel the need to please, because they've been conditioned to be compliant. As a result of these reinforcements, we are more likely to see women behave in a compliant way. They come in on time, they get their work done to meet deadlines, and they are not as likely to rock the boat. Meanwhile, men tend to be less concerned about their behavior and more concerned with their ideas and getting credit for good solutions. So while we may not consciously choose to act one way or another, the conditioning we experienced at younger ages influences us, and it also influences the way in which we perceive others. One could argue that we are more likely to label women with words like "bossy" because we have been conditioned to think that leadership in women is not the norm. If we are compliant, it's difficult to lead. Leaders often emerge when they identify a new path forward, not when they tell people how to behave. Likewise, when we see a man behaving in a nonconforming way, it is no different than we might expect. So we have to undo our unconscious wiring that makes us act certain ways, and label ourselves and others.

How to Consider Unconscious Bias and Self-Advocacy as You Start Up

How does unconscious bias relate to starting up? You need to ensure that you can advocate for yourself and be aware that you will face unconscious, if not outright conscious, bias as you work to launch your own enterprise. This skill transcends industries and is really one that can be applied throughout your career path. So if you're still in a traditional job, it's worth practicing. And if you're ready to make the leap into entrepreneurship it's important to identify and remove some of the subconscious learnings that can get in the way for women.

For example, studies show it's not enough to ask for a promotion: how you ask also matters. If you complete all the work that's been asked of you and then ask for a promotion, you are not likely to receive it because the perception is that you simply did a good job. However, if you start the year by saying, "I'm confident that I'm capable of leading even more teams and taking on more responsibility. I'd like to leverage this year to showcase my capabilities, and I am asking that I be considered for a promotion with additional responsibility," you're more likely to be taken seriously. It's not what you did but rather what you are capable of doing in the future that leads to promotion.

The same premise applies to starting a company. What you do today builds your credibility. What you plan to do makes your business something of which people and investors want to be a part.

While you can start a business with next to nothing, as you progress you may want to consider raising capital or seeking funding sources. When starting a business, women often wait until they are much further along to ask for capital than men. In a later chapter, we'll cover some of the additional external issues that make raising capital more difficult for women, but at this stage, it's important to understand that the desire to do a good job, while valuable, isn't a sole factor in helping you progress. Like the classic fairy tale of Goldilocks where one bowl of porridge was too hot, one was too cold, and one was just right, the same holds for how and when you seek funding or the next validation for your pathway. If you wait too long, you're cold; you may be perceived as trying something for too long, or simply being satisfied with your current role. If you ask too quickly, you're hot; you may be perceived as hasty or unwilling to prove your credibility. It's challenging, of course, to find that perfect temperature, but the goal is achievable. A way in which to do it is to think about each project, job, or effort you are working on as one of value. You'll need to be able to point to your accomplishments as evidence of your ability to deliver, but it will be equally important to demonstrate that you have the ability to take on expanding goals and responsibilities over time. In short, you need to erase any conditioned "need to please" mindsets and showcase not only what you can deliver, but what you plan to deliver and how you will crush those goals.

It's not just in the act of fundraising that women experience the impact of unconscious bias, though. In customer meetings, especially with older, more established companies, many executives will assume that a woman is the assistant or more junior person on a team rather than the CEO.

Take, for example, the idea that there are two types of unconscious bias—descriptive and prescriptive. As described by Madeline Heilman in her article "Description and Prescription: How Gender Stereotypes Prevent Women's Ascent Up the Organizational Ladder," there are different terms we as a society use to describe categories of people. Women are often described as helpful, kind, and sympathetic, while men are often described as aggressive, forceful, independent, and decisive.

Moreover, we also view these traits as oppositional, meaning that if we think that a certain trait belongs to one group, we assume it doesn't belong to the other group. So when we observe a non-conforming behavior in women or men, we view it as wrong or unusual. It's easy to understand why traits associated with leadership then are viewed as negatives when possessed by women. We've been conditioned to assume there is something wrong with the woman if she behaves outside the preconceived norm. Just as striking, of course, is that when men exhibit behaviors that society is more likely to label as feminine, they are perceived as weak or ineffectual, even if those "feminine" traits make them better leaders or managers.

In line with this is the more recent interest in showing that the very biases we associate with leadership may in fact be faulty. Studies show that while people who possess traits like assertiveness, independence, and so on, are more likely to rise to the top of organizations, the best leaders are often decisive but empathetic. This means that while men who tend to exhibit certain characteristics may be more likely to be promoted, we're not promoting men and women who might actually be more effective leaders. Thus the goal to get more women into leadership positions should not discourage men from continuing to pursue them too. Rather, we have an opportunity to rethink what traits we want in leaders and how they impact company and team performance.

In Chapter 4 we'll cover more ways that you can leverage some of these perceived weaknesses into strengths.

I Didn't Always Have This Figured Out

Earlier in my entrepreneurial journey, I went to a fundraising event in New York City. I had left my small children home with husband. I was dressed in a knee-length pencil skirt, a blouse, and low heels. I had my business cards on hand, and I was ready to give an elevator pitch about my company on a moment's notice. My husband and our two young boys were back at home in the suburbs getting their pajamas on, and I was at a small event in New York designed to help entrepreneurs connect with investors. I had gone to the event optimistic about my odds, given that my software company was showing some traction. But once I was there, I found it harder than I thought to meet people, and I sort of went from one person to the next introducing myself, having a few minutes of small talk before the next conversation kicked off. I was one of only a few women at the event, so I felt slightly self-conscious, but no more so than I had working in tech before I had the kids.

And then I heard, "Hey, you, are you handing out badges? Can I get one?" Suddenly my confidence took a dive. I realized that this person thought I was the "badge girl," not an entrepreneur. I had already felt slightly self-conscious, but I suddenly felt like a fraud for being at the event. I turned around quickly to regain my composure, and another attendee turned to me, clearly a few drinks in, and asked me to share my pitch. When I did, he looked at me and said, "you know I like your idea, but you're just not enough of an asshole." Completely rattled, confused and irritated by these judgments, I made my way to the ladies' room to get my thoughts together. Given the dearth of women at the event, the women's restroom was a pretty quiet place to think. I realized that this event was not likely to produce any positive results for my company, and I was having a hard time not taking all of these comments personally. I remember straightening my shirt and looking in the mirror to tuck my hair behind my ears and regain my composure before heading back out to continue networking. I had to remind myself that I was the CEO of my company. I wasn't even sure what he meant by saying I wasn't enough of an asshole, but I knew it wasn't meant to be a compliment. But I knew, then and now, that I couldn't let these judgments impact how I thought of myself, and years later I've decided to take his insult as a compliment.

Many years later, I understand more about what happened that night. We all hold subconscious biases, and when we meet people we typically just categorize them in whatever image we have of a role. We think of CEOs of startups as white, young men in hoodies and, as an example, we easily see teachers as women. And just as some of those people clearly underestimated me, I was also likely projecting self-consciousness. I was prepared for the night, but I wasn't beaming confidence, and I didn't have any strategies for handling it. (You'll learn more about converting those per- ceived weaknesses into strengths in Chapter 4.)

Similarly, years later when I had started a company and we secured office space, I gravitated to a small office in the back of the space. A junior salesperson I had hired asked for a different office, and I had no issue granting him the corner office. I never felt that I was there because of status. But a few weeks later, one of my board members arrived, and had a very direct conversation with me. He told me to take the corner office, and said that I was setting the wrong tone by selecting the one I had. I recall questioning him about it, and he bluntly let me know that people would not assume I was the CEO if I didn't take that office. I ulti- mately moved, and know that he was correct. I chose the lesser office because I unconsciously didn't want to make waves, and my gender only reinforced the idea that I wasn't the one in charge. Moving to the corner office took care of any misperceptions. I didn't need to explain who I was to visiting guests. They could make the assumption based on my office position. Obviously I would prefer that this didn't matter. The reality was I liked the office that was tucked a bit out of the way down the hall. But the perception that others had of me did matter at that point, so the move was worth it.

Why Affirmations Matter (Yes, You Can Is a Good Example!)

Studies indicate that a key to success in leadership is also simply the affirmation of success as a possibility. Our natural tendency as humans is to look for what's wrong. It's a survival mechanism developed through evolution to protect us from harm. The small internal voice that says things like "come on, you can't do that" or "it might fail" or "don't rock the boat" or "what makes you think you can do this." is there to protect you from harming yourself. We each have thoughts that run through our heads, that make us nervous to approach new topics or meet new people or try new things. The negative thoughts are unique to each person, but are there to in some way keep you safe. If you're part of a group that has traditionally been lesser represented in certain roles or experiences, it is logical that your internal dialogue might be more negative to protect you from the great unknown. That's why I think affirmations can be incredibly powerful resources to help you achieve your goals, and why I called this book *Yes, You Can Do This!* and not something less affirmative like *Women Can Give It a Try*.

An affirmation is simply a statement that can be written, expressed internally, or said out loud. As we practice reminding ourselves that we are capable, and others provide more images of what's possible, I think some of the unconscious bias will start to melt away. At a macro level, we all have affirmations before us all the time that remind us of the potential for men and, in particular, young men, to succeed as entrepreneurs. Flip to the cover of any industry publication, and you'll likely find that image of a young guy in a hoodie disrupting industries. I remember as an elementary student seeing Steve Jobs in his classic 1980s red suspenders on the cover of a book, and being intrigued by this rebellious example of success. But when society hasn't put forth any images or affirmations of what success can look like for a group that's different, whether by gender, race or ethnicity, it's harder to relate to those images.

So creating affirmations becomes a way to instill confidence and the potential for success before society shows it to you. For example, the author Scott Adams, of *Dilbert* fame, has written extensively about how he writes down new goals 15 times a day to affirm that they are possible. Most famously, when he was not yet a successful cartoonist, he wrote, "I, Scott Adams, will become a syndicated cartoonist." Obviously he did become a famous cartoonist. As he's noted multiple times on his blog, it's not that he considers the act of simply writing down the affirmation the reason for his success. Rather, as humans we're often either allowing negative thoughts to circulate in our minds or we're unconsciously soaking in the limitations that society is broadcasting. By consciously writing down affirmations of what you want to be or do, you're putting the positive thought to the forefront of your thinking long enough for it to become a constant reminder of what is possible. As internalized messages or societal messages are replaced, our outcomes actually shift.

For example, there are studies showing that when women comprise more than 17% of a group, the idea of being a "token" woman dissipates, and people start to view the group as simply that, a group of people. This shift in perception allows people to focus on individual contributions rather than isolate someone for a unique character trait. A perfect example of this in play are the dynamics happening in the 2020 U.S. presidential election compared to the 2016 race. In 2016, Hillary Clinton was the sole female candidate in the later stages of the Democratic primaries, and ultimately the Democratic nominee for the U.S. presidential election. Throughout the campaign, her wardrobe was critiqued as she dressed the part with pantsuits. In 2020, with more than five female candidates running for the nomination, wardrobe has become less of a topic. In fact, the degree of variance in dress has increased, but the attention on the candidates as women has decreased. One could argue that Hillary's presence on the national stage led others to picture themselves there. And as they saw themselves there, they didn't feel a need to dress in a more masculine outfit to blend with the other men. Instead they could dress as individuals, and be on stage simply as candidates. As we see more of ourselves in our leaders, we can find easier paths to enter new areas.

While the statistics continue to point to a low number of women in leadership positions in corporate environments, we risk continuing to believe that it's difficult or impossible for more women to hold those positions. So until society starts showing women more images of successful women, we need to hold the image for ourselves and believe in our own possibilities, or it will be impossible for anyone else to. When you're told that the CEO and the administrative assistant are entering the room, what do you picture? It's easy to imagine a middle-aged man as the CEO along with his much younger, female assistant. But I'd challenge you to check yourself the next time such a thought enters your mind, if in fact it does. Actively take control of your thoughts and picture the opposite. By thinking the new thought, you actually will shift your response, and you might do more to unravel many of these constructs we take as truth by subconscious default.

Additional Questions to Consider

- When you enter a conference room, do you sit at the outside boundary of the room?
- When you are leading projects, do you describe your work by saying "we do," rather than "I do"?
- Do you often apologize to make others feel comfortable, even when you haven't done anything wrong?
- Do you ask for what you think you're likely to get, rather than what you really need or want?
- Do you avoid sharing updates with your boss, so as not to appear like you're bragging or troubling her or him?

If you answered yes to these questions, you are likely partially hindered by your own internal unconscious bias. The following are a few simple activities to regularly try to undo these patterns.

Simple Actions to Take That Can Help Shift Perception

- When entering a meeting room, if possible, sit near the center of the boardroom table.
- Practice using the phrase "I did" instead of "We did." If you are a leader, you obviously had a team working with you. As a leader, it's important that you recognize the contributions of others and attribute success to the team. However, it's just as important to be able to claim the work that you individually did as your own.

- Don't apologize. Full stop. If there is a dispute or conflict, don't apologize unless you actually have something to apologize for. We have a tendency to apologize to make everyone comfortable.
- When making an ask, think big. Don't aim for what you think you could get, aim for something much higher than you want. This gives you room to negotiate.
- If you have a boss (and later, when you have a board), make sure you're "managing up." Regularly send updates that keep him/her informed.

You can do this!

Why to Consider Meditation and Gratitude as an Additional Resource to Build Esteem and Generate Confidence

Meditation is a hot topic in popular culture right now. At its core, I think of meditation as a way to calm the engine that is the brain long enough to allow one to more easily control thoughts and their related emotions. Just as I shut off my computer to allow it to get updates and charge, so too do I actively seek to calm my brain to allow it to recover. This process also allows you to banish intrusive thoughts from your mind and to clear the subconscious rhetoric and messaging you may be unknowingly carrying around with you. If you are worried about others' attitudes or struggling with what others may think you can use your meditation time to clear your mind and regain your confidence.

While there are many articles on the benefits of meditation, which include reduced stress, increased memory, and reduced anxiety, many people struggle with how to meditate. I believe that if you are in a less mentally stressed state of mind, you will be in a stronger position to claim your good.

As authors Deb Shapiro and Ed Shapiro pointed out in the book *Be the Change: How Meditation Can Transform You and the World*, meditation can help you develop confidence because by quieting your mind, you'll become more aware of and more likely to embrace who you are.

During the process of meditation you begin to label thoughts as just those—thoughts. You then begin to disassociate those statements or ideas from your own sense of self and get to the root of who you are, connecting with and creating a sense of self-worth and trust. The idea, at its core, is that if you identify a thought as separate from who you are, then you cannot be that thing. So if you find yourself thinking a negative thought during meditation and let it go, you are in fact letting that negative, limiting belief go.

The process of meditating also permits us to become more aware of our connection to others, to our planet, and to all of the things that are happening. As we start to understand the inherent good and self-worth in ourselves, we more easily recognize it in others.

There are a number of different ways to practice meditation.

The following is a routine I follow each day in the early morning.

1. Find a quiet room where you will be undisturbed for at least five minutes. (This can even be the bathroom if you need a lock!)
2. Sit down, legs in a criss-cross-applesauce position.
3. Set a timer on your phone for three to five minutes, so you avoid immediately wondering how much time you have left to meditate.
4. Close your eyes, and visualize being in a completely empty room with no windows or doors.
5. Choose one word that you find generally calming (examples could include Love, Abundance, Joy, Peace, Harmony, etc.).
6. Focus on your breath. As you breathe in, say the word in your mind, then breathe out.
7. Continue mentally saying that one word in alignment with your breath.
8. If a different thought pops up, simply acknowledge it as a thought and let it go with your breath.
9. Continue focusing only on that one word until your timer goes off.
10. Begin to visualize the doors and windows of your quiet room opening, and allow the people and things you value the most to come into your space.
11. Express gratitude for those things, and open your eyes and stretch to rise.

This simple exercise takes just a few minutes, but can significantly help rest your mind for the day ahead. By clearing your mind, you literally give your mind a chance to reset and cool down. By ending the exercise with an expression of gratitude, you force yourself to seriously consider that which you already have.

By taking this step, you actually create a stronger foundation on which to move to the next place. Have you ever encountered someone who complains frequently? They talk about how they can't stand their job or their boss or their spouse. While they seem to be approaching life from a point of wanting change, their focus on what they don't want actually leads them to talk about their problems, and it becomes difficult to envision the positive thing they will actually accomplish. By learning to express gratitude for what you have, you will find that those things will become more a part of your conversation with others, which in turn could lead to new opportunities you hadn't thought of yet.

There is also science to support the idea that gratitude leads to more success for men and women. Benefits of gratitude, which have been highlighted by multiple studies and touted by authors including Amy Morin, a contributing writer with *Forbes*, and Nataly Kogan, author of *Happier Now*, include improved self-esteem, increased empathy, improved self-esteem, and physical health. The idea is that by expressing gratitude for what you already have, you are elevating your own sense of well being, and in turn elevating your appreciation for others. This provides an opportunity for enhanced creativity, connection with others, and an understanding of what others may want or need.

So as you're working to consider entrepreneurship to build the life you want, take a moment to affirm what you are capable of, look for positive images that match your goals, meditate to clear and expand your mind, and remember that a little bit of gratitude goes a long way on your professional journey.

Chapter 4

Your Perceived Weaknesses Are Your Hidden Strengths

How to Leverage Your Weaknesses to Start Up

What you'll take away from this chapter:

In this chapter, we'll explore the ways in which your perceived weaknesses can actually be leveraged as strengths. Traits that are generally assigned to one gender or group are often perceived as oppositional to the other group, and are therefore considered abnormal for the opposite group to possess, but that doesn't mean that those traits are without value. Rather, it means that how we assign them is off. After reading this chapter you'll walk away with some clear responses to questions you may get, and a new approach to consider your own self-assessments. In addition, we'll also look at some practical advice for the most challenging situations.

When It All Goes Wrong

"So ... I went to a local venture meet-up downtown. I think it was a disaster." Maria still looked a little shaken as she described the experience. Maria and Jill were meeting for coffee.

"Oh, what happened?" Jill asked, curious and empathetic, as she wrapped her hands around her cup. "You're not fundraising right now, right?"

"No, I was just going to the event to learn more about the industry and network, but I just—I don't know. I got there, and felt ready to talk to people about what I was working on, but I actually felt like the token female. Like people were humoring me, but not really listening to me." Maria had been so excited to meet other entrepreneurs and investors, and shuddered as she thought of how overwhelmed she had felt the night before.

"Well—let's go through it. You know I hear a lot of board-level pitches in my current role. You may be overthinking it." Jill had a lengthy career as a head of product for a Fortune 500 company, and was accustomed to helping to craft and review executive-level pitch decks.

"Okay... so I registered weeks ago, because the event was advertised as a fantastic networking opportunity, and I thought there might be some investors as well as potential customers there. It was downtown at the We-work space. I made an effort to look smart but artsy or entrepreneurial, and wore my black capris, low heels, and a mock turtleneck shirt, but you know I still feel a little self-conscious from the extra baby weight...." Maria tugged at her sweater.

"Okay, first of all no one cares about that, and you know you look fine—but what happened...? Why did you think it was a disaster?" Jill took a sip of coffee and looked directly at Maria, with the goal of getting to the facts.

"Well, I got there as the speaker was starting, so I grabbed a seat toward the back. And then I started looking around and realized that I was one of the only women there. It was mostly men, looking pretty casual. I almost felt like I was intruding, so I had trouble jumping into networking when the break-out started. When I would finally get someone's attention, and share what I was working on, I would just hear "that's nice.

"Then when one of the investors started to engage, he immediately started asking me how I planned to deal with the risk. And of course I explained it to him. I said how actually companies are already spending millions on this type of solution, and the risk has always been there."

"Hmm . . . let's try another way." Jill recognized the pattern that Maria was describing, specifically that investors tend to ask questions that send women down a path of risk management, whereas they ask men questions about the size of the opportunity.

"What do you mean?"

"How about—Well—like any large market opportunity, it's important to think about how to mitigate risks. I've already done that by researching x, y, z. That step is really going to allow me to get hold of this market in a much bigger way going forward.

"You've seen Capital One, Equifax, and others all fail at security...my training solution will be the one of choice for every CEO or CIO worried about being the next one. We've thought about risk so they don't have to, and they are already demonstrating that they'll spend money for it."

"But it wasn't just the risk issue—one investor asked me how old I was. When I told him, he was like—oh, you're pretty inexperienced to handle such a big market problem."

"Ugh—that's so obnoxious. How did you respond?"

"I said, well—Zuckerberg was pretty inexperienced as a 20-something working in his dorm. Jobs was pretty inexperienced trying to figure out the market for the personal computer, and then—get this—the investor actually said, 'oh, but they were incredibly ambitious.' As if I was somehow getting the worst of their traits! I was inexperienced *and* I wasn't nearly as ambitious."

"This is just so irritating." Jill recalled reading a study on this type of behavior, but recoiled as she heard about it happening in action. She furrowed her brow as she thought of how Maria could have approached the conversation that might have led to a better outcome.

"Perhaps you could have started with leveraging all of this as a strength?"

"How?" Maria was exasperated. "What do you mean, leverage all of this as a strength?"

"Well, we know from studies that this is a frustrating unconscious bias people have that leads them to perceive women with exactly the same qualifications differently. There was a study I read about in the *Harvard Business Review* recently that investigated the ways in which investors treat males versus females. And while the results are irritating because they point to exactly the type of conversation you had, there may be ways to leverage them to your advantage."

"Jill, it's hard enough to raise capital—I'm not sure what type of mind games I now have to play on top of it." Maria inhaled deeply, trying to compose herself. She wondered if Jill was a little out of touch from her corner office … Surely she didn't know what it was like to be out in the wild, trying not only to get your company off the ground but at the same time trying to raise money.

"Maria, let's try an exercise that you can use when you are ready." Jill wasn't really sure if all of these techniques would work, but thought it was worth a try.

Let's Role-Play!

"Okay, let's try a role-playing exercise. You pretend to be the investor. I'll be you. And let's see how it goes." Jill was actually excited to test out her theory.

"Hi, it's great to meet you." Jill reached out to shake Maria's hand.

"Okay … you as well." Maria glanced down at her Apple Watch, mimicking the distracted attitude she had dealt with last night.

"For the 200-billion-dollar market that is underserved by shoddy, old customer service software, I've developed a unique solution that will disrupt the entire industry." Jill tested out Maria's pitch.

"Oh, okay … " Maria started playing along more seriously and took on the flat tone of the people she had just met. "Well, that's a nice idea, but how are you going to deal with all the potential security risks you're introducing to a stressed industry?"

Jill rolled her eyes, realizing what Maria was mimicking, and quickly grasped the narrow line of questioning Maria had just experienced, but took a stab at a better answer.

"Well, all companies are going to have to manage the types of security risks you're talking about, with or without my solution. That's why there's no better time to dive into this market, which has a 500-billion-dollar opportunity in the first three years." Jill crossed her arms as she finished her response, feeling good about how it had come together.

"Jill—I *wish* I had said that! That's such a better answer than the one I gave, which was 'gee—let me get those stats for you, and show you how I would do it.'" Maria realized that she could have flipped the awkward conversation with that investor on her own.

"Great—let's keep going!" Jill had been reading about these types of behaviors, and was genuinely excited to help Maria on her quest to build a business.

"The thing is, once you get your business off the ground, you can really forge your own path, but it's also helpful to understand how to counter some of the challenges you'll face along the way. Think of it as working with the system to eventually change the system."

* * *

You Really Are Perceived and Treated Differently

In the narrative, Jill was citing information presented in a 2018 study that *Harvard Business Review* covered. It showed that investors are more likely to perceive men and women with the same skills and experiences differently. Moreover, they tend to ask men and women different questions, and then perceive them differently in response.

Men were more likely to get questions about the size of the opportunity they were going after, whereas women were more likely to get questions about how to mitigate risk.

This makes it more difficult for women to convey why they are onto a large market opportunity. In addition, the study showed that when answering the same question, men were perceived as young, but ambitious while women would be perceived as young and inexperienced.

While in a perfect world we would get all investors to simply change their questioning, I am confident that if we can help women react with this knowledge in mind, we might make more of an impact.

In this one example highlighted in Jill's conversation, redirecting the answer to get to the larger opportunity is a way to convert a perceived weakness into a strength. In one answer, you have not only addressed the size of the opportunity, but you've also demonstrated that you understand and are managing the risk. This could actually make you more fundable.

Other attributes commonly stereotyped as being more female include multitasking, politeness, and sensitivity.

Although certainly not all women have these characteristics, many are perceived as having them. So knowing that you may be perceived that way, what are some ways you can leverage them to your advantage?

CEOs need to be able to juggle multiple priorities and understand their entire organization. In fact, most successful CEOs have had experiences across industries, in sales, engineering, and operations, rather than in one tight vertical. Your ability to manage multiple tasks at once lends itself to that type of leadership position. If someone were to make a statement like "oh, you must be really good at multitasking," you can respond by saying, "Yes, like all great leaders, I am able to juggle multiple priorities and view challenges from multiple points of view." Don't let someone imply that your work, or their cultural perception of it, has a negative slant.

Likewise, studies show that companies that put their customers first outperform other companies. If you are given a hint that you're perceived as polite, then you can respond by saying, "Yes, I am. That's what makes my customers value my product, and I expect no less of my employees."

Perceptions are an unavoidable part of life, but knowing that all people are perceived ought to help you prepare for the offhand comment or direct question. You can't change a first impression based on perceptions, but you can respond in a thoughtful way.

Goal Setting as a Framework for Success versus Perfectionism

Perfectionism is another trait that many women are stereotyped as having. The word itself sometimes lends people to think it could be a compliment to be considered a perfectionist. But perfectionism is really not completing something until you feel it's perfect. Despite the sound of this word, it is a known weakness, because the implication is that one who is seeking "perfect" will not finish a project on time or will belabor it when resources could have been better spent on something else. You can undo this perception by proactively demonstrating your competence in completing projects on time. In fact, you can set your own goals long before you have investors or any type of stakeholder, and then report on them to employers, investors, board members, or your teams on a regular basis. This demonstrates that you can meet and exceed deadlines without defending your process.

Another perceived weakness is simply being the only woman in the room. Studies do show that when a woman is alone, she is more likely to be focused on as "the woman." Once a sizable mass is achieved, being a woman becomes a nonissue. So if you're going to an event for networking, consider recruiting other women to come with you. That dynamic will help you feel less conspicuous. However, if you can't bring anyone, try to remember that you can use this to your advantage. You will stand out as being different, so people will be more likely to remember you afterwards when you do follow up, networking via email or LinkedIn. If you experience doubt or fear, simply remind yourself that you belong there because of the work you are doing. Visualize that you are in fact in a winning circle, and that people will want to help you.

You can do this!

Answering Questions That Are Rooted in Unconscious Bias

Table 4.1 shows some questions and comments that you may hear as you forge your own path. In fact, many of these are questions I've received over the years. The responses may be useful to you.

Table 4.1　Answering the Questions Differently

Question	How to Respond
Have you really thought this through?	Yes. Would you like to see my five-year model?
But what about security? There's a lot of risk out there.	The size of this opportunity is so enormous that I have taken a considerable amount of time researching security implications and ensuring that any risks are easily mitigated.
Do you really think you have enough experience to take this on?	I know I have the right skills and experience to take this on. Certainly many of the most well-known entrepreneurs out there have had far less real-world experience.
You know, you've got some competition out there.	Of course; I've done a full competitive analysis, which I'd be happy to share with you.
When is your boss arriving?	I am the boss.
You look nice today.	Thank you.
Do you think you're ambitious enough for this?	I wouldn't be here talking with you if I wasn't.

Tracking Goals

As you define your monthly or quarterly goals and track against them, you are creating a narrative that you deliver on time, on budget, and are capable of using investment dollars wisely. You can start tracking whenever you decide to start your business, long before you have any employees or customers.

Table 4.2   Example of Goal Accomplishment Tracking

Q1: What we set out do to	What we did in Q1
Design and develop responsive user interface	Designed and delivered responsive user interface
Set up hosting in AWS	Set up hosting in AWS
Survey at least 100 prospective customers	Surveyed 200 prospective customers and leveraged feedback to enhance design
Gain at least 1,000 new customers	Gained 1,500 paying customers

You can add to and update a chart like this on a quarterly basis. This type of resource will not only help you hold yourself accountable for meeting the goals you set, but it gives you a framework to describe your successes to others.

The Elephant in the Room: Sexism, Bias, and Harassment

I would be remiss if I didn't call out that in the workplace, women not only deal with the effects of unconscious gender bias, but we sometimes deal with the very real bias of sexism as well.

I recently interviewed Eula Scott Bynoe, host of the critically acclaimed podcast *Battle Tactics for your Sexist Workplace*, and heard first-hand how the issue is still impacting women across industries. The impact can range from feeling obliged to clean up after office meetings to being judged more harshly for exhibiting emotions to dealing with unwanted advances from peers or managers. I won't take a ton of time to cover this topic, as I think it warrants a deeper analysis and is a topic that people experience individually, despite the recent #metoo movement.

What I can say is that in an ever-changing landscape, it's important to understand when you're dealing with unconscious bias versus full-on harassment. If your job is threatened, if you're dealing with unwanted advances, or if you're being attacked, you are dealing with behaviors beyond uninformed, unconscious bias.

If a superior or someone in a position of power (an investor, a manager, etc.) behaves inappropriately, I recommend calling them out on their behavior in clear terms and then reporting the behavior if necessary as soon as possible. However, I also appreciate that every situation is unique, and it doesn't always feel possible to deal with issues head-on.

I recommend first labeling the behavior and then expressing how you interpreted it. For example, you can fill in the blanks on the following: "When you just said _____, it made me think you meant _____. I'm not comfortable with that, and wanted to give you a moment to clarify your request/statement."

Try not to let it fester, debate how to handle it, or gossip about it. Making it your focus only ruins your time. Be firm in your response and hold the person accountable. For example, you could say, "I'm surprised and disappointed that you would behave this way. I trust that you don't make your decisions this way." The person will likely be shocked and embarrassed that you confronted them, and quickly work to move on. At that point you can also report the behavior if you choose to do so.

Then go back and focus on your business, and look for someone else to support you. Try not to spend another second worrying about it. I write this not in an attempt to sound dismissive. Rather, I write this to encourage you to feel empowered to think about the types of people who would say horrible things to you as no different than how you would view a mentally ill person on the street begging you for something. By choosing to move on, you empower yourself by not feeding into their world-view. However, if you decide that the behavior was particularly egregious, or they actually did block a job or opportunity for you, then I encourage you to say something.

Many organizations have safe ways to report behavior. In a corporation, you can of course, bring an issue to your human resources team. If you encountered this type of behavior at an event, try to reach out to the event organizer. If you ultimately choose to not say anything, then own your choice and move on—not because you excuse the behavior, but because you decided that you are not going to let someone else's attitude impact your path forward. Those types of people are simply not worth your time or energy.

Section II

Building for Scale and Avoiding the Traps: Debunking the Myth That Women Don't Think Big Enough

Good business leaders create a vision, articulate the vision, passionately own the vision, and relentlessly drive it to completion.
—Jack Welch, former chairman and CEO of GE

Chapter 5

You Might Have the Next Big Thing

Your Experiences Are Different Experiences Than Others'

What you'll take away from this chapter:

In this chapter, we'll explore the ways in which you can be innovative. Innovation is sometimes misunderstood to be a single product. In reality, there are many opportunities for innovation and therefore businesses. In this section you'll learn about the different types of innovation, examples of women who have built successful companies based on innovative approaches, and questions you can consider to think more constructively about innovation.

Innovation Is a Broader Term than You Might Think

"I guess I've never considered myself a creative—but I have lots of ideas on improvements that could be made around this place." Sitting on the playground bench, Sophie wrapped her hands around her knees.

"We sort of have this misconception that you have to be like Edison to be an innovative person, and that doesn't really hold up." Carolyn, another mom from the neighborhood, rifled through a diaper bag as they talked. Carolyn was also a stay-at-home mom but always had a side project coming along. She had occasionally joined the meetings at Jill's house, but knew Sophie more closely from their experiences on the playground with kids.

"Right—exactly: I always feel like if I'm not coming up with the next personal computer, that I'm not really on to something. I've been so inspired by the meetings in our group to launch businesses, but I'm not really sure what's worth pursuing. I know I need to think big, but at the same time many of the things that are interesting to me seem kind of trivial. You know—I'm not an engineer working on the next lightbulb."

Sophie noticed Jack, her four-year-old, hanging upside down precariously on the monkey bars and rushed over to catch him.

"Right—like how about an inflatable trampoline to whisk at the kids when they do crazy stuff like that!" Carolyn laughed as she watched Sophie dive under Jack, tripping on the way down.

"Ha, now that would be an innovation!" Sophie wiped her forehead, laughing, while Jack ran off to the swingset, oblivious to the near-catastrophe he had just created.

"I'm convinced that there are plenty of opportunities for businesses. I mean heck, look at soda. Who would have thought that the maker of bubbly water would be one of the largest companies in the world." Carolyn stood up to guide her younger daughter off the slide.

"You mean Coca-Cola?" Sophie was pushing Jack on the swing.

"Right—every time we talk about startups, I feel like people are looking for the next Facebook or Amazon or something. And I totally get that, but some guy who thought to carbonate water back in the 1800s created a company that makes billions a year. I feel like there are so many ideas out there. You just need to land on one that makes sense to you."

"Right—I guess I also feel like sometimes I'll just be labeled a mompreneur." Sophie realized she felt bad as she said the term in that way.

"What do you mean by that?"

"Well—sometimes I hear stories of women who started companies, and it just sounds like they made some trivial toy or diaper widget, and that it's not as important as other companies. I think they mean it in a good way, but I always feel bad when I see an article highlighting mompreneurs—like they are somehow less than other 'regular' entrepreneurs."

"Yeah—I hear you. I don't think that's how the publications mean it, but that's part of the challenges we all face as women.

My advice would be to not worry about how you might be perceived and just own what you're working on. There are actually some amazing stories of women who started their own companies based on unique challenges they had."

"I feel like we never hear about those. I can't even think of one." Sophie scratched her head, literally trying to think of a famous female entrepreneur from her school days.

"Right—of course not, because schools only seem to mention them when it's Women's History Month or something."

"Ha—even better, most of the ambitious women I remember reading about usually also met untimely deaths." Sophie jogged her elementary school memory.

"Oh my gosh—you're right! Madam Curie . . . Joan of Arc . . ." Carolyn starting laughing as she thought about how absurd it all was.

"Amelia Earhart! All the amazing women who dared to venture on their own, and their untimely demises!" Sophie chuckled. "Everyone we were told about had a weird cautionary tale about them."

"Exactly, but there have always been women doing amazing things, and in particular I know there have been awesome women entrepreneurs—"

"It's just that many of the companies they built were for problems they had that may not have seemed huge—but they were."

"Who are you thinking of?"

"Well, take the inventor of white-out."

"White-out?"

"Right—the inventor of white-out was single mom from Texas who was working as a secretary. She sold her company for over $45 million."

"Or SPANX! Did you know the founder of SPANX was a regular woman who realized that she liked the way she looked better with control-top pantyhose?" Carolyn asked.

"Oh wow . . . I hadn't thought about those . . . and I love my SPANX." Sophie thought about how obvious it now seemed that a woman had invented the undergarments that had literally held her together after her second child was born and she had had to wear an evening gown for an event.

"Listen, I'm not saying that you have to invent SPANX or white-out, but I think you probably have ideas to offer because you're a woman."

***

Seeing What's Possible

As you heard from Carolyn and Sophie, sometimes we stop in our tracks because we think that we have to have a groundbreaking technical solution to start a company, or that we're not real businesspeople if we're creating solutions from our experiences as mothers or women. But that's not the case. There are many stories, which we seldom hear, of women who have built businesses, and they serve as examples for what's possible.

In this chapter we'll first take a look at some of those women who were successful entrepreneurs and what they built.

We'll also unpack the different types of innovations and how you can think of them as you work to consider creating your business.

For starters, as Carolyn and Sophia discussed, because women have not been in positions of power in traditional corporate environments for very long, the list of successful women entrepreneurs is obviously shorter or less well known.

But as discussed in the first section of this book, one way to help more women see a path is to show more examples of what's possible.

While I've included snippets of my own personal experience throughout this book, I think it's worth sharing some examples of very successful women who started their own companies.

Identifying Types of Innovations

Before we jump into some examples, it's important to understand the types of innovation that are possible and could potentially warrant the creation of a new business.

Innovation is simply described as the creation of something new. But there are multiple types of innovation to consider.

Incremental Innovation

An incremental innovation is an improvement or enhancement to a known product or solution. For example, Cherry Coke would be defined as an incremental innovation to Coke, which was already successful in the market. Incremental innovations tend to cause you to purchase more of a new thing, but are not necessarily disruptive of the original. Other examples of incremental innovations include the electric typewriter, the automatic shift car, the reclining chair, Jibbets for Croc shoes, the upside-down ketchup bottle, and the strapless bra. There are countless examples, but for each of them, the end user did not change, but the product had an incremental innovation, which either caused more customers to purchase it or allowed the company to continue to compete.

Disruptive Innovation

A disruptive innovation is one that disrupts an existing business entirely. For example, Uber, a multisided platform, mobile service designed to help people easily obtain a ride from one destination to the next as well as empower people to become drivers, actually disrupted the traditional taxi business. Uber enabled people to get a ride whenever and wherever they wanted, and it removed any need to have a payment method on hand since the app saved the user's credit card information. Uber also allowed anyone with a driver's license to earn income as a driver at whatever times they wanted to, and in a vehicle of their choice.

In just a few short years, Uber, and its subsequent competitors like Lyft, created an easier method of transportation for would-be taxi customers, and created a new income model for people. It's been particularly stinging for traditional taxi drivers, because anyone could give a ride and it disrupted the need to apply for and purchase a taxi medallion, which often costs over $100,000.

Other examples of disruptive innovations include the automobile, the personal computer, the iPhone, e-commerce, online content streaming sites like Netflix, and marketplace sites like Airbnb. In each case, the new innovation, whether it was a new technology, business model, or service, disrupted an existing way in which customers achieved their goals. For example, the automobile eliminated the need to use a horse and buggy, Netflix eliminated the need to go to a physical store like Blockbuster to rent a movie, and sites like Airbnb disrupted aspects of the hotel business.

Innovative Business Models versus Innovative Solutions

It's tempting to think of innovations as products, like the iPhone or microwave. But in reality some of the biggest innovations have been those to a business model or go-to-market strategy approach. As Parker, Van Alstyne, and Choudary highlighted in their groundbreaking book *Platform Revolution: How Networked Markets Are Transforming the Economy—and How to Make them Work for You,* many of the companies that are currently disrupting the Fortune 500 are not product companies; they are platform companies. Uber, Airbnb, Amazon and PayPal each disrupted the way in which customers connect with each other, rather than relying on the creation of a single product. Each of those companies created a platform with which to engage, rather than a one-off product to sell.

Likewise, Netflix's original product wasn't disruptive to Blockbuster. But its business model was. Rather than relying on the late fees of customers to drive revenue, Netflix found more ways to make it easier for customers to avoid late fees, moving from an at-home delivery of DVDs to an in-home streaming service.

In 1994 Blockbuster was the largest distributor of video rentals for home use. There were physical stores around the country, where consumers could easily rent movies, and the company was valued at $8.4 billion. In 1997 Netflix was founded and quickly saw growth by providing an online service to rent movies with at-home delivery.

In 2000, Blockbuster had an option to purchase the entire company for $50 million but turned it down, choosing to try to compete with Netflix instead. But with changes in management, Blockbuster neglected to grow its online business as quickly as Netflix did and by 2010 Blockbuster's valuation had decreased to $24 million while Netflix had a staggering $65 billion valuation in 2017, which had resulted from their successful business model innovation.

The point is that while product is key, disruptive innovation can happen.

Why Diversity of Viewpoints in Innovation Leads to More Innovation

It's been well documented that diversity in leadership leads to better performance and increased innovation. Research shows that firms with diversity across their networks generate more product innovations. But it's worth paying attention to the fact that the research shows that companies with diverse leadership teams actually have stronger top-quartile performance and more innovative products. Research from a recent *Harvard Business Review* article described how companies that had both inherent diversity (gender, ethnicity, sexual orientation) and acquired diversity (studying abroad, diverse experiences, etc.) within their leadership team were more likely to report that their companies captured new markets and grew. The thesis of the article is that companies in which diverse voices are represented are more likely to relate to more diverse customer bases, unlock new innovations, and budget for more ideas.

I think this is worth highlighting for a few reasons as you consider building your own company:

1. Your diverse and unique experiences as a woman do truly increase the likelihood that you'll develop a service or solution that could be disruptive.

2. As you work to build your team, it's worth keeping this research in mind so you remember to surround yourself with people with diverse points of view.

3. While women are traditionally underfunded compared to men in investment circles, I think studies that show that more diversity leads to better performance will ultimately convince investors to diversify their own portfolios. Logically, investors want to maximize their returns, so if that means investing in more diverse founders, then it's reasonable to believe that at some point they will view diverse portfolios as more valuable than more homogenous portfolios.

As we explore some examples of past and present women entrepreneurs, it's easy to comprehend why their diverse experiences and viewpoints led to innovations at scale that others in more traditional positions may never have conceived of.

The following section highlights some examples.

The Creator of Liquid Paper (White-Out)

And so women have to just keep on with their determination and be relentless. We have to not relent.
—*Bette Nesmith Graham, as recorded by the Business Archives Project in 1977*

The name Bette Nesmith Graham is not one that that students tend to learn about in traditional school settings.

But she's actually a perfect example of a successful entrepreneur who happened to be a woman, and a single mom, no less. In the early 1950s, when women could still be hired or fired based on their sex, had no basis for maternity leave, and could not gain a line of credit without a male signatory, Bette Nesmith Graham was a single mother in Texas working as a secretary to earn a living. At that point, she earned just a few hundred dollars a month, equivalent to approximately $2,000 per month in today's dollars, and had no career progression opportunities beyond rising to a higher rank of executive assistant. As a secretary, one of her main responsibilities was to type letters using the instrument of the day, which was a typewriter. The personal computer we're all familiar with now would not be introduced for decades. At that time typewriters did not provide a simple way to delete mistakes beyond trying to erase them, and secretaries were assessed by how well they were able to quickly type without errors.

As Bette worked, she became frustrated by how difficult it was to erase a mistake when she was preparing documents. According to interviews, that frustration led her to think of another way to remove mistakes. A former artist herself, she was inspired by a painter who was working on a large sign across the street. Bette noticed that, as he worked, he did not try to erase a letter he had painted incorrectly. Rather, he simply painted over it. That led Bette to realize that she could fix her typing mistakes by covering them up rather than erasing them.

That realization, which sounds so simple now, was incredibly innovative. Bette spent years working on paint formulations in her kitchen and garage, and even got assistance from her son's chemistry teacher. The story goes that she eventually started putting her mixture into nail polish jars and selling it to fellow secretaries, who were eager to use the new solution. She became completely consumed with building her business, and she was eventually fired by her main employer for putting her company name on a letter instead of her actual employer's. But like many entrepreneurs, that led her to double down and build her business in earnest. She went on to apply for a patent for her solution, and eventually she developed operations in Europe and the United States, selling more than 25 million bottles a year.

Moreover, she built a company with corporate structures that were progressive at the time. For example, she included onsite childcare, a library, and a greenhouse. One of her core company values was on putting the quality of the product over profits, and permitted more democratic decision-making across the organization. She also established a foundation in support of women in the arts. Bette's story was not without challenges, though. At one point in her journey, she remarried and then went through a bitter divorce, during which her husband attempted to have her removed from her own company. She ultimately persevered and sold the company to Gillette for more than $45 million.

An Incremental Innovative Sales Strategy That Created a Different Way to Sell: Tupperware

It's easy to think that only great inventors can be entrepreneurs, but often it's the a creative innovation in which goods are sold or produced that leads to success. Take for instance, Brownie Wise. Brownie Wise was not the inventor of Tupperware, the plastic food storage containers popular to this day. However, she was the implementor of the sales model that led to the success of Tupperware, which had over $2.2 billion in sales in 2016.

Until 1950, Tupperware, which was created by Earl Tupper, had had little or no mainstream success. Brownie, who had been in sales for Stanley Home Products, identified a path to market for Tupper. She built upon the direct sales model that Stanley Home Products used, and created Tupperware Home Parties LLC with Tupper. Brownie expanded on the initial direct-to-home model, and added "jubilees and sales conventions."

The model of having in-home parties to see an offering where homemakers could also make an income was innovative and led to long-term success. The central idea was that homemakers could have parties where they saw first-hand how durable the product was, had the potential to make an income, and socialize. The model has been used in other successful enterprises such as Mary Kay Cosmetics and Arbonne.

While Brownie and Tupper eventually parted ways before Tupperware was sold, she is a classic example of an entrepreneurial woman who innovated around a business model rather than a product.

An Incremental Product Innovation That Created a Billionaire: SPANX

In 1998, Sara Blakely, the founder of SPANX, cut the legs off her stockings so she could be comfortable at a party while still having a control top for her figure. She realized she was on to something other women would want and started working on ways to bring her idea to market at scale. Two years later, in 2000, she found a manufacturer in North Carolina willing to make her product. The U.S. hosiery industry at that time was still predominately male-owned, and many manufacturers didn't understand the value of her innovation. That year, Sara made her first sale to Neiman Marcus by trying on clothes for the purchasers with and without the undergarment to show how much better their customers would feel and look wearing SPANX. By the end of that year, her product was featured on *The Oprah Winfrey Show* and quickly took off. By 2012 Sara was listed as the world's youngest self-made billionaire. She's now also publicly pledged half of her wealth to charity.

Her story is exciting because it shows that innovation that can impact an entire industry doesn't necessarily require an advanced engineering degree. Rather, Sara identified an opportunity based on a unique experience that she was having, and, of course, realized that a subtle adjustment to her undergarments could lead to a multibillion-dollar company that could impact every single woman who suffered from the same challenges she faced.

A Disruptive Business Model Innovation: Rent the Runway

Just as Brownie Wise's innovative sales strategy led to the growth and adoption of Tupperware and Sara Blakely's modification to traditional pantyhose led to SPANX, so did Jennifer Hyman transform the way in which consumers get their more expensive dresses with Rent the Runway.

Rent the Runway is an online ecommerce site designed to let users rent, rather than purchase, clothing. The central idea is that customers can rent a designer dress for four to eight days at a very low percentage of the retail price. The rental includes the necessary dry cleaning and physical stores in some locations, which include access to personal stylists. This model is completely disruptive to traditional retailers, and one that others hadn't considered.

Jennifer founded the company in 2009 and has grown the business to over 11 million members and more than 1,800 employees. Moreover, in 2019, the company closed a $125 million round valuing the company at $1 billion with Bain Capital and Franklin Templeton as lead investors, while Hyman was nine months pregnant. She not only brought the sharing economy to the fashion industry, but she created a company where a high percentage of the staff is female and the entire executive team is comprised of females.

To my point, by stepping into leadership positions via entrepreneurship, women can automatically take hold of more leadership positions as their companies expand and succeed.

Turning Reviews into a Viable Business Model

Even though I started a company, I didn't picture myself like that.
I wasn't a big idea person.

—*Angie Hicks Bowman*

In 1995, Angie Hicks Bowman was a recent college graduate working as an intern for Bill Osterlee. She'd been asked to help him find a reliable construction contractor. As she made her way through the process, she realized how difficult it was to be able to tell who was reliable or not. So she started to scour the local community, to see if people would be willing to give reviews. After 1,000 door-to-door visits, she'd gotten x number of signups. She then pitched the VC for funding to turn her reviews into a business. By 1999 they were on the internet, and by 2011 she had over 11 million users. Angie's List was acquired by HomeAdvisor in 2017.

When asked by *Entrepreneur* in 2017 what inspired her, Angie said, "My family. My kids. It's why I do what I do, it's for them. Being their role model and their support is everything to me."

Was this an incremental or disruptive innovation? This innovation was taking the way people normally discovered things—with reviews—and flipping it to something people wanted.

A Makeup Artist Takes on an Entire Industry

Huda Kattan was born in Oklahoma to Iraqi-American immigrants. As the middle of three sisters, she's said in numerous articles that she spent a significant portion of her childhood following the beauty habits of her older sister and experimenting with makeup on her younger. While she majored in finance in college, she studied makeup after her graduation, and ultimately landed a job as a makeup artist, working on celebrities, including Eva Longoria and Nicole Richie, and later started a blog called *Huda Beauty*, where she shared makeup tips.

In 2013, frustrated by the lack of false eyelashes to meet her goals, she designed her own, and launched her own cosmetics line with just a $6,000 loan from one of her sisters. She's gone on to garner a tremendous following on social media, was declared one of "The 25 Most Influential People on the Internet" by *Time* magazine, and in 2019 her company was valued at over $1 billion.

* * *

There are numerous stories of women who have successfully built businesses because of their unique experiences, rather than in spite of them. While some certainly had ample income or wealth before starting, and others rose up from near obscurity, it's clear that it was their individual unique experiences and perceptions that led them to success. Twenty years ago it was perfectly acceptable to write off an actress as "just an actress." But today we're seeing countless examples of women who have courageously built upon their brands to offer new services, including Gwyneth Paltrow, Reese Witherspoon, and Jennifer Lopez.

My Own Experience

I'm certainly not a celebrity or a billionaire business mogul. However, I do have experience creating innovative solutions and hope my story will shed a little more light on what's possible for everyone, whether you're currently struggling to make ends meet or simply wishing you could do something more creative.

The first product I came up with was a direct result of my own experience as a new mom. When my children were babies, I knew that I wanted to create a traditional baby book for each of them, in which I could capture photos, track milestones, and jot down their experiences. This was just around the time that Facebook was going live, and there were limited online services of the sort available. So my idea was to create a website (which I realize now, in 2019, seems pretty basic, but at the time it was novel) to easily allow parents to track milestones, journal, update photos, and convert to a printable book. My husband jumped in to help with software development, and we got to work. The site was called Little Chapters, and the idea was that each month in a baby's first year was a small chapter in their bigger story. Within a few months of launching the site, we had thousands of users, were featured on some mom blogs, and I'd negotiated a contract with an on-demand book publisher for fulfillment.

In hindsight, I would have been smart to simply stick with this concept and work on monetizing it. Instead, I started to look for other markets that might have a faster path to revenue and would require a similar service.

I went to multiple conferences, and stumbled upon an opportunity in the early childhood market. It turns out that teachers had to track similar milestones for young children in their programs, so we started to work on how to modify the software to accommodate multiple children in one class, which was actually similar to the idea of multiple children in one family from a software perspective.

That led to many more meetings and conversations, and ultimately to a friend who was an early childhood consultant and deeply understood the field of early childhood accreditation. Through conversations and research, we learned that many early childhood centers had to track these types of milestones and activities if they wanted to maintain their status with a national organization called the National Association for the Education of Young Children (NAEYC).

With that information, I realized that we had identified a reason for people to not only use our software, but to be willing to pay for it. Our service would ultimately save them time, reduce the use of paper, and save them money, so they could spend more time focused on the children in their classrooms. This realization led to strategic meetings with NAEYC, and, after nine months of negotiation, a contract relationship to be authorized as a certified resource for their community and members.

That innovative approach to improve a process that teachers and administrators were required to perform led to opportunities in additional markets, including higher education and K–12, before we were acquired by one of the largest educational content providers in the country.

Once under the larger corporate umbrella, I took on the role of Head of Labs, which was a unit designed to foster and create digital innovations for the company. We had the freedom to develop, move quickly, and ultimately quickly move on from solutions that didn't work. Over the course of just a few years, my teams built an Amazon Alexa app to test the idea of a computer-simulated teacher, an API program designed to allow third-party developers connect with and engage with content, a marketplace site designed to support innovators in educational content and included users including teachers, Google, and Microsoft, and an internal tool for ideation. I was fortunate during that time to be able to take a course on innovation at MIT and to work closely with experts in platform economics and data science.

What I've learned over the years is that the best innovations often come from problems you or your customers are facing, and are usually made better through collaboration, diversity in viewpoints, and the willingness to pivot.

You can do this!

Questions to Ask for Innovation

As you consider what innovative business or product you should create, you can use the following questions to guide you.

- Is this problem one that impacts multiple people?
- Is this really a problem, or is it a "nice to have"? (e.g., is a painkiller required, or would a vitamin do the job)?
- If this solution were to take off, which, if any, businesses would it disrupt?
- If this solution were to take off, would it complement other businesses? Could there be potential partners?
- How easy would it be for a potential competitor or current industry leader to copy this solution?
- Why isn't anyone else doing this yet?
- Am I interested enough in this problem to spend the next five years working on it?
- Can I easily define the types of users my solution or business would serve?

An Exercise in Innovation

Some of the innovations with which we are most familiar started by combining two existing items. To stretch your creative thinking, look about your surroundings, and think about what new resource or solution you might come up with by combining existing items.

For example, what could you create:

- With the power of a stove and a dishwasher?
- With the light of a lightbulb and the accuracy of a thermostat?
- With the mapping app of Google and a survey of restaurants?
- With a camera and a database?
- With a brush and a comb?

What other items can you think of that might take on new meanings when combined with others?

Chapter 6

Build Your Confidence by Writing Down Your Future

How to Develop and Use a Business Plan as Your Personal Playbook (and to Combat Imposter Syndrome)

What you'll take away from this chapter:

In this chapter, we'll explore the ways in which writing down your ideas and constructing a business plan can help you not only think through your plans, but will help you build the confidence to execute them. Many women struggle with imposter syndrome, and this chapter will help you combat it by writing down your goals and how you can achieve them.

Getting Back to Sophie ...

Sophie pulled the strap on her bag in an effort to balance it on her shoulder as she walked into her local Starbucks after dropping the kids off at school. Maria's face was glowing from the glare of her open laptop, clearly already hard at work.

Since her conversation with Jake, Sophie had found herself thinking about Maria's conversation more regularly. She had a notebook of some ideas she was collecting but wasn't ready to pull the trigger yet, so she had been excited when Maria offered to meet her for a coffee downtown to talk about it. Sophie walked over and tapped her on the shoulder.

"Oh hey!" Maria pulled her earphones out and smiled.

"Can I grab you a coffee?" Sophie put down her bag on the wooden chair across from Maria.

"I'm all set—I've been here for a while." Maria smiled warmly, and Sophie exhaled, realizing that Maria was genuinely happy to jump into a conversation.

"Okay—I'll be right back." Sophie was glad the line was short at this hour and rushed to the register to order her coffee.

As she put the lid on her to-go cup, she glanced at her phone to double-check the time. She had about an hour before she'd have to leave to get her youngest from preschool. Preschool for three-year-olds was just three hours in the morning, so after the 20-minute drive to the school and the 15-minute wait for pickup, Sophie only had about one hour to fully engage in another activity. On many days, that hour was used for household chores, so she was feeling energized to meet Maria for something completely different.

Sophie pushed her bag to the floor as she pulled the chair out to sit down.

Maria closed her laptop and smiled warmly, laying the earphone cords on the table.

"Hey—glad you could meet. How are things?" Maria had taken a few vacation days to work on her young business, but was happy for the company.

"Great—but since our last conversation, I haven't been able to stop thinking about potentially starting my own business. How is yours going?"

"Yeah—it's intense, but I'm excited about the possibilities. Like I said, I'm not ready to quit my day job yet, but I'm making real progress. Rather than going on a trip this year for vacation, I actually booked a vacation to work on my business. It's kind of liberating to be at home this week hanging out here." Maria gestured broadly across the room.

"It's so inspiring! I have a few ideas for a business, but I'm not sure if I'm ready to jump in. Things are already pretty stretched." Sophie thought about her last conversation with Jake.

"Well—why don't you just start by putting some ideas to paper? You could start by putting together an executive summary of what your business could be. Not many people will ever read it, but it's a great way for you to organize your thoughts." Maria opened her computer again, quickly searching for an example from her work, and turned it to Sophie to show her the example.

Sophie glanced at the screen, noticing the title for Maria's company at the top.

"Got it—yeah—I had been browsing articles on the web about this, and I saw a lot of conflicting info. Some sites said to write a full business plan. Others said not to bother and just write an executive summary."

"Here's the thing: If you go down this path, this company is yours. Who you share or don't share your plan with is entirely up to you. And likewise, who reads your plan is totally up to the people with whom you share it." Maria closed her computer again and slid it into her bag before pulling her own drink closer for a sip.

"So you're saying I should just start writing?"

"Yes. Look, before I got started I thought through several ideas. But I found that in order to really feel clear about the best direction to go, I needed to put my ideas to paper. A business plan forces you to think through all the parts of your business—the product, the market, your competitors, your hiring needs, and so on. What you plan today may not be what you ultimately implement, but I like to think of it as my own living document I can reference to see how I'm doing."

"Got it—I have a few ideas I can dig into. After I get one done, would you mind if I showed it to you? I'd love to get some feedback. I'm pretty isolated from a business perspective at home right now."

"Of course—but you know, you may even want to start at a level above a business plan."

"A level above? What does that mean?"

"Well—you could start with a vision board."

"A vision board? Isn't that one of those woo-woo things people do for self-help or teenage girls put on their bedroom walls?"

"Maybe—but I like to think of it as a way to get my highest objective together first. It's sort of like this: Your vision is where you're going, while your plan is how you get there. So, for example, if you want to go to Boston, you first say, "I'm going to Boston," and then you go figure out how to get there. Not the other way around.

"Try thinking through where you really want to be in a year. Are you doing what you're doing right now but with a little extra income? Are you in an office, with 20 employees making an industry disruption? I'd start by really thinking about what you want and grabbing some pictures to help you visualize it." Maria was refreshingly pragmatic.

"Once you have that, you can start thinking about which idea is most likely to get you to where you want, and develop the business plan or action plan to get there."

"That does make sense ... I can't build a plan if I don't know where I really want to go and what I want my whole life to look like."

"Exactly." Maria leaned back in her chair and crossed her arms, nodding.

* * *

Standing Up for Your Business and Fighting Imposter Syndrome

In the investment community, there is often discussion on whether a business is a lifestyle business or if it's a venture-backed business. To clarify, a lifestyle business is one that will potentially fund your personal lifestyle. It could produce just a few thousand dollars or hundreds of thousands of dollars, but it's not designed to scale exponentially, whereas a business that could be backed by venture investment needs to be able to scale exponentially. As examples, Facebook was a venture-backed business because it's a solution that could be used by everyone in the world, whereas a small consulting business is likely a lifestyle business.

I will tell you that in my limited experience, I've only encountered women who have been asked to defend whether they are actually creating a lifestyle business while they are actually working to raise capital for what they believe is a scalable solution. While there is nothing wrong with a lifestyle business, by default it's harder to get investment to support one, and the very questions of whether it's a lifestyle business or not again puts women on the defensive about the size and scale of the opportunity they are creating.

Moreover, many women suffer from "imposter syndrome." Originally described by psychologists Pauline Clance and Suzanne

Imes in 1978 as a condition wherein people feel that they aren't really worthy of the success they have achieved, the term has become a staple in conversations about women in business. Many high-achieving men and women suffer from this syndrome, which is rooted in the idea that any success is a fluke or luck. The syndrome, while not a disease, is a mindset that can cause people to stop before they get started. Feeling like you don't deserve the success you have makes it difficult to defend or articulate where you are going.

By crafting a detailed business plan, you can document your goals and your plans to get there and treat it as a living document to recall your successes along the way. By maintaining this type of document, you can remind yourself that, in fact, the outcomes you are achieving are no fluke, dissolving any opportunity to discredit yourself and taking away the opportunity for others to do so. I also sometimes refer to this practice as the data dump. If you can build enough of a data set to prove to yourself that you know what you're doing, you'll build the confidence to do so.

Making Your Vision Concrete

In this chapter's narrative, Maria also mentioned starting with a vision board. A vision board is often used in self-help books and other resources, with a goal of getting deep clarity on the life that you want. Many people create vision boards on sites like Pinterest or, more traditionally, they may actually make a physical board by taping magazine pictures or postcards to make it easy to remember and visualize their goals. For example, sometimes when people are working to lose weight, they will put a picture of a thinner body up on their refrigerator to remind themselves of why they shouldn't grab that extra ice cream.

In *Forbes* magazine, columnist Eilene Zimmerman described the results of a study that TD Bank did in 2016 on the impact of visualization for entrepreneurs. In short, the study showed that approximately two thirds of business owners think that they can more easily map and develop their business plans by using visualization of goals. Of business owners who used a vision board or similar tool, 76% claimed that their business was where they had originally envisioned it using the technique. And a whopping 82% of business owners who used a vision board early on reported that they accomplished more than 50% of the items they placed on the board.

I'm confident that you can also use a vision board to help define what you truly are seeking. It's the bigger "why" behind the company. You're not just starting a company to solve a market problem. You're starting a company for autonomy, for freedom, for a better life for you and your family, as well as to support of your company's strategic mission. Perhaps you have a burning desire to create a company that will automate the delivery of healthy meals to people in need. Before you write the business plan, you may want to include an image of well-nourished children on your board. Perhaps you are working on the next Uber- or Lyft-type business. You could include pictures of content people driving cars on your board. The vision board is not a tool that you will share with external people. It is a tool you can use to clarify your own vision of what you are working to build, and easily remind yourself of why you started this project in the first place.

As you progress in your business, though, you may convert some of these images to professional shots that you can leverage to enhance your office environment and remind employees of why they are there. Knowing that younger workers are more likely to work for a company that has a core set of values or a mission makes it important to remind yourself and your teams what your deeper purpose is.

Whether you opt to make a digital vision board or a physical one, here are some steps to consider that I've used in my own experience.

1. Map out what you would like your entire life to look like in five years.
2. What mission are you working on?
3. Are you and your family healthy and happy? Are your team members happy and healthy?
4. Are you traveling? If so, where? Paris, London?
5. What does your office look like?

6. Do you have a certain amount of money in your bank account?

7. Are you running a large organization with hundreds of people?

8. How are you dressed? Are you wearing a suit and in a boardroom, or are you wearing casual clothes with flipflops?

9. Is your company in the press?

10. Are you working one-on-one with people in consultative work?

11. Are you attending conferences?

There are no right or wrong answers to any of these questions. But getting very clear about what your ideal life looks like will help you as you consider the type of business you want to start. Take some time and close your eyes, and really picture the life you want. I also find it helpful to visualize after meditation.

This will help you determine the type of business you want to build. Once you have clearly captured what you want, start looking for pictures that capture that visualization. You can create categories for business, career, family, spirituality, health, volunteering, and so on, and then place the images that relate to each under that category. Whatever life you want, there is a business you could build that would get you there.

Developing a Business Plan

Maria's advice to Sophie is correct. Most investors won't necessarily read through a full business plan. However, many government agencies or grant funding sources will insist on them. A business plan is really just a detailed documented designed to clarify the problem you're solving, why it matters, and how you will execute the solution. In a world where women still face unconscious bias and are often challenged on the merits of their work and the size of the opportunity, crafting a business plan can help give you the confidence to easily answer questions about what you are working on.

Whether you're working on a small consultancy or a potential venture-backed enterprise, the core components of a business plan are the same:

> Start with an executive summary. Your executive summary should cover at a high level what your business is and why it should exist. At this stage, just focus on writing a brief summary of your intended business in one to two pages. Let the reader understand the name of your business and why it should exist. What is your product or service? Who is your customer and why? Who will be running this business, and why are they (you) qualified to do so? At a high level, who are you going to be competing with, and why would someone choose your business instead of the competition? How much will it cost to run your business, and how much money will you make?
>
> The rest of the business plan is basically a deep dive into each of the following areas and is intended to serve as a guide as you think through each of the components of the business needed for it to be successful.

Industry Analysis

Provide an overview of the industry in which you are building your business. Are you planning to build a business in the education industry? The retail industry? The cybersecurity industry? Regardless of the industry you choose, you should be able to define what it is, how large it is, and why it needs your business.

Market Analysis and Competition

Within this industry, what is your market? For example, you may be building a business in the education industry based on a growing trend that you've identified. Is there a certain segment of that market you are working on, such as K–12, public schools, private school, or universities? Within those market segments, is there a particular customer you are targeting, such as teachers, administrators, students, or parents? The more specific you can be in defining how you'll tackle specific segments and customers, the more realistic you can be about the specific market opportunity size you are working on. You'll also want to research and define who the competitors are in this market. It's sometimes tempting to say that your solution is so innovative that there are no competitors. If this is the case, there may actually be no market. So spend some time looking at current patterns of behavior in the market: Are there companies that could easily step into your space? Are your potential customers leveraging a different process to achieve similar goals today? What is the overall competitive landscape? One example to consider is Uber. When they initially launched, their competition included traditional taxi companies and other traditional transportation services like buses and personal cars. They were bringing an innovative service to a market in which there weren't any companies providing a similar service, but they were competing with existing, entrenched behaviors. When Lyft launched after Uber, they were competing directly with Uber itself, so their competitive benefits had to be articulated differently. Your competitive landscape will change and evolve over time. Documenting it in your business plan should not be an effort to set it in stone. Rather, it's an opportunity to continually assess and reassess those that are going after the same market as you.

Your Sales and Marketing Plan

This will evolve over time as you learn more about your customers and competition. However, it's helpful to try to answer the following questions: How will you reach this market? What is your digital marketing plan to gain leads and customers? Will you need salespeople? If so, will they be outside reps who travel and build relationships to develop large accounts? Or will they be inside sales reps who mainly respond to inbound leads with product depth? How much revenue should each salesperson bring in, and how much will they cost to hire? How long will it take you to hire each rep, and how long will it take you to ramp them up? What other strategies will you leverage to cultivate business? Will you be attending conferences or events? Will you be doing any advertising? Will you be leveraging social media influencers? Will you be working on an SEO (search engine optimization) strategy?

If you plan to advertise, what is your anticipated ROI (return on investment)? In addition to answering these questions to build out your sales and marketing plan, you'll want to make sure you're tracking customers and potential customers in a manner that empowers you to make a forecast of what could be sold over time. See the resource section of this chapter for an example of a sales pipeline.

Your Management Plan and Ownership

In this part of the business plan you can describe in more detail the type of business you're starting. Define the business structure as an LLC (limited liability company), a S Corp, a C Corp, or a 501(c)(3). Describe why you selected the corporate structure you did. You'll also need to describe who is managing the company, what their roles are, and what percentage of the company they own.

Your Operational Plan

This is the section of the business plan to describe your physical and operational needs. Will you have an office space? Will you need facilities to manage inventory? Will you be running a virtual business, leveraging the cloud? What will your hours of operation be? Will you provide 24/7 support to customers? What components are critical to ensure the operational success of your company?

Your Financial Plan

We cover this in more detail in Chapter 7, but you'll want to build out a model that shows how you will spend capital and generate revenue. You'll create a model that outputs an income statement, a balance sheet, and a cash flow statement.

Your Appendix

In this part of the business plan, you'll put any additional information that could be helpful to someone evaluating the business, such as additional market research, marketing collateral, resumes, references, and so forth.

How My Business Plan Helped Me

I can tell you that when I was working on my business plan, very few people ever saw it. However, when I was asked for it, it was critical to have it. Before I raised any outside capital for my business, a member of the local entrepreneurial community, who I met at an event, did ask to see my business plan. He in turn advised me to submit it to a local university competition, which resulted in gaining a summer's worth of free MBA services to help me with my pricing strategy. For three months, three MBA students studied my plan, analyzed my market, reviewed my solution, and provided feedback that confirmed I was on the right path along with suggestions on ways to improve. Following that experience, I somewhat routinely updated my plan over time, and years later it was always a requested document during due diligence for larger investments and during the acquisition. So while you may not need one, it can come in handy, and it will help you feel more confident in the plans you are verbally sharing with others.

You can do this!

Developing a Vision Board

In the following figure, you'll see some images that reflect various goals I've worked on over time, including landing a podcast on Apple's New & Noteworthy list, enjoying a concert, traveling overseas, and speaking at a conference. You could easily create a board that includes your target market, outcomes from your five-year plan, and actual dollars you plan to achieve in revenue. It's simply a visual reminder of what you're working towards.

Sizing Up the Competition

As you document your potential or real competition in your business plan, it's helpful to place them on a quadrant chart as shown below. This helps you easily describe the areas in which you are specifically competing with them, and it enables someone learning more about your business to quickly determine where your company fits. Are you better on cost, quality product, and so on?

Quadrant View

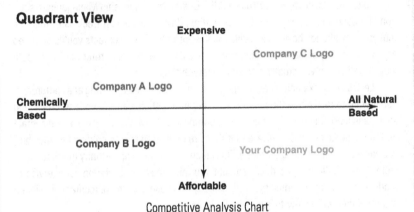

Competitive Analysis Chart

In the feature comparison view (see the following example), you continue to show how you compete, but rather than just laying out four areas of strengths or weaknesses, you compare at the feature line. It's important to realize that features can change—the company that is hard to use today may improve and be easy to use tomorrow. But the feature comparison chart empowers you to really show where your solution stacks up.

Feature Chart Comparison View

	YOUR Company	Company A	Company B	Company C
Cleans all surfaces	x	x	x	
Safe for wood	x	x		x
No harmful fumes	x		x	x
All natural plant based	x			x
Inexpensive	x		x	

A feature comparison chart is another way to show how you compare to your competition

Understanding the Sales Pipeline

As you begin to sell a solution, it's important to keep track of what opportunities you have in your pipeline. A sales pipeline is simply a snapshot of the potential customers you have and the likelihood that they will buy your product or service. This information becomes critical for you to predict what your future growth is and becomes part of your business plan.

To break this down, you can use a CRM (Customer Relationship Management) solution like Salesforce or Hubspot. In your earliest days, you can just track all of this in a tool you may already have, like Excel. You'll want to track any contacts you've obtained and whether they came to you from conferences, your website, or referrals. Then you'll mark whether you've actually made contact with them.

Let's say, for example, that you get the card of someone interesting at a conference. You'll want to take down the person's relevant information, name, company, email, and so on, and mark them as a contact in your database or CRM. Once you make real contact with them again and they indicate that they are interested in your product and may buy, you can mark them as an opportunity. This means you have an opportunity to sell to them. From there, you'll assign a dollar amount you think they will spend on your service or product, the month you think they will actually purchase, and the percentage likelihood you think they will follow through on all of this.

Let's say a potential customer says, "Yes, I will buy this, now that I've seen a demo. But I won't have money to do so until next month." You could mark them as 50% likely to purchase on whatever date next month is. Now let's say it's the next month, and they ask you for a formal quote to process the order. Now you can flip them to 75% likely to close. Once you've actually signed the contract, you can flip to 100% closed and won. Alternatively, let's say her budget disappeared and she said she no longer wanted your product now, but would take a look again next fiscal year. You would change the date to the next fiscal year, and move her down to 25% likely to close.

Over time, these types of steps will serve as a predictive mechanism to determine your potential revenue on a monthly or quarterly basis. For more information on how to manage sales as you start a business, see *Sell More Faster* by Amos Schwartzfarb (Wiley).

Sales Pipeline Terms

Lead	Prospect	Opportunity	Stages of Opportunity	Win/Lose
Leads are simply the contact information of potential customers. Companies often find leads through conferences, inbound web traffic, and referrals.	Prospects are qualified leads. In short, this means that you reviewed a lead, and verified that it is a real person, at a real company, with the purchasing power to buy your solution.	A prospect becomes an opportunity when you make contact with the prospect, and confirm that indeed they want a solution like yours.	As you work with the opportunity, you mark them at the likely percentage they will actually order, and assign a dollar amount and projected date of close. (For example, you may move a customer requesting a demo to 50%. A customer ready to get a contract may be at 75%.)	As you move opportunities along, you may learn more and move them up or down in percentage. If you close a deal, they are won at 100%. If you lose the deal, they are lost and back to 0%.

Basic Sales Terms and Content You Need to Know

Chapter 7

Tell a Bigger Story

Don't Apologize for Thinking Bold

What you'll take away from this chapter:

In this chapter, we'll explore the ways in which you can craft a larger story and justify that it's possible to achieve it. You'll develop skills to overcome a preemptive need to apologize and find resources to help you clearly document what you plan to do, how to get there, and feel confident along the way.

Is Your Story Big Enough for Investors?

"Jill, it's funny—I was just helping Sophie start to think through her business plan last week, and I realized that mine must have a gap in it." Maria was curled in one of Jill's plush chairs, with a throw blanket over her lap. She was excited to have these regular meet-ups with Jill and the other women to talk through professional and personal challenges.

"What's making you think that?" Jill was very far along in her career, and was glad to be giving back by mentoring some of the younger women in the community like Maria.

"Well, remember that event that was a disaster—where I was so upset about being treated a certain way?"

"How could I forget?" Jill rolled her eyes as she recalled the challenging conversation that Maria had had at the investor event. Jill was at a stage in her career where she genuinely enjoyed helping others think more deeply about how to forge ahead. She knew that one of the strengths that experienced leaders have is pattern recognition. Over the years she'd encountered plenty of uncomfortable conversations and seen the traps that less experienced professional can fall prey to. Her experience empowered her with a broader perspective, she understood how things moved through cycles, and was able to limit her emotional response to a given situation.

"Well, I've been processing it, and I think maybe there was a sliver of merit to some of the conversations. While the role-playing with you really helped me think about how to reframe some of the questions I was getting, I am now wondering if I wasn't telling a big enough story in the first place."

"That could be. One of the challenges I've seen people have is not being able to articulate just how big of an opportunity they are working on. You know, while you know and totally get that you have this massive opportunity, you might be just sharing the narrow vertical you're in today." Jill was interested in Maria's approach but also saw how Maria sometimes thought bigger than she talked.

"Exactly. I feel like I'm in the weeds with the few customers I have ready to buy my software today, and I am having a hard time sharing my vision of how big this could be with others." Maria had analyzed the market and knew that she could really scale her business but struggled with articulating the potential without seeming like she was stretching it.

"Well, before you start trying to convince everyone how big it's going to be, have you tried writing a press release?" Jill probed.

"Um—Jill, I haven't officially launched yet. I'm still in beta with a few customers in my spare time, so why would I have made a press release?" Maria was sometimes surprised by Jill's questions.

"Sometimes it's helpful to write a press release *before* you launch. It actually forces you to get crystal clear about the value you're creating and why it matters." Jill had seen people at her own company use this method, and also knew many others had touted the model, including companies like Amazon.

"Maria, if you *were* ready to go live, what would you want the newspapers or press to pick up?

"You mean, like, what story would I want them to tell the world about me and my company?"

"Exactly—let's start with just the headline. What could it say? Obviously, they are not going to write a story about how a young woman from Indiana is creating software that's currently kind of clunky for one or two companies." Jill raised her eyebrow, prodding Maria to think harder.

"Oh, that is an interesting exercise. I guess it could be something to the effect of 'Starboard Enterprises Announces Revolutionary SaaS Platform, Positioned to Disrupt $10 Billion Industry.'" Maria smiled as she finished the sentence.

"That's a good start! Now start to think about what else you would want them to know . . . What is the platform? Why does it matter? How many customers would you have?" Jill leaned in to the conversation, intentionally working to draw the information from Maria.

"I think I see where you're going with this . . ." Maria sat back and grabbed her pen and notebook.

"Right. You want to imagine the most exciting positive outcome that could come as a result of all of your work, assuming you were properly funded and had great execution. Solidifying that story of success will help you share how big your story can be with others." Jill had experience working with the corporate communications team at work, and knew that press releases were often drafted well in advance of the anticipated outcome. That advance effort often drove work and conversations in a way that an arbitrary deadline might not have.

"My recommendation would be to take a stab at that press release. You don't need to share it with anyone, but you can really start to think about the features that matter and visualize the massive opportunity you're seizing. It's going to have to be to be newsworthy, right?"

Jill heard the doorbell ring and jumped up to let in a few of the others she had invited over, while Maria started writing voraciously. Jill was energized by the momentum this monthly gathering was creating.

* * *

Putting the Press Release Strategy to Work

Later in my career, when I was heading up a product development team, I used the press release as a tool to clarify where we were going and keep individuals on track so we could meet deadlines without sacrificing the ability to iterate and be agile during the development cycles.

When I kick off a project I know it's important to make sure everyone is aligned on what we are building, why we are building it, and what the most important outcomes are.

In any large-scale project, it's easy to lose sight of the goal because individuals can get in the weeds.

For example, if you are working on building a new software solution that will empower executives to easily track and manage budgets across multiple business lines, you will want to ensure that team members stay focused on that outcome versus getting bogged down in unnecessary details. By creating a press release to which everyone can align their work, you can help keep people on track without micromanaging them. For example, let's say that your press release announces the launch of your "[new online product] that is [already in use by [several large customers], and easily [allows executives to securely view and download reports] [across multiple projects] to [improve efficiencies in the company] on September 15."

What features are included in the statement?

Let's break it down. (1) We know from the sentence that the solution must be available online. (2) We must already have several large customers. (3) The solution must have a way for an executive to securely log in and view and download her reports. (4) It must be available by September 15th. That's really all the statement calls for. With these goals, we can make sure the developers are working to fulfill the core product needs, that the product development team is clear on what each of those should look like from a user-experience perspective, that the sales team is building relationships and selling to large customers, and that everyone knows that September 15th is the drop date.

Where I've seen people slow down, or get in the weeds, is in overdeveloping what other features could be part of a solution. Certainly in this case, numerous features could fit under that statement, like the color of the reports, the other people in the company who could have access to the reports, the level of interactivity within the reports, the interoperability of the reports with other systems the company uses, and so on.

But by using a press release as a guiding framework to development, your team can easily ask themselves, "Will this feature I'm suggesting make our press release more or less true? Will we be able to announce the launch of this product on September 15th if we don't have a secure login but we do have a purple version of the report?" Of course the answer is no. The press release clarifies for the team what is mission critical. Although software will always be improved and iterated upon over time, knowing what's essential to announce helps keep everyone aligned.

A Brief Example

To make this more specific, imagine, if you will, that it's 2015. When I was heading up a Labs development team I learned that the C-suite team wanted to explore the development of a marketplace or platform offering. The CIO asked me to run the project, which was completely outside the core business and would therefore have little initial understanding within the company. To get the project off the ground, I started by researching the type of marketplace that could work, and developed a relationship with experts in the area of platform strategy to ensure we were considering all the potential implications. I then created a visual of the type of team I would need to build and deliver it. This was a multifaceted initiative that required a complete set of capabilities including software development, data science, business development, customer support, marketing, and event planning.

The first step in this project was not to build; it was gaining budget approval to move forward with the project. In large companies, even with C-suite backing you still need to build your model and justify why budget should be formally allocated. For me that meant selling that vision of the final goal, and the team it would require, back to my boss and the board of directors.

From there, after the team was up and running, I had to sell the vision to those working to build it. How would the software engineers understand what to build if I couldn't articulate the vision? As a head of product for the project, I drafted a deck of what a completed platform could do, who would use it, and the impact it would have. That vision became something we could all hold on to over the weeks and months it took to not only build it, but simultaneously onboard users of the site ahead of launch. Within a year, we had launched with thousands of resources on board, no downtime, positive news stories, and an award for cool new tech solutions.

Own Your Ideas with Confidence

When you're explaining your big idea to investors, other entrepreneurs, or even people in your company, it's sometimes tempting to apologize in advance. What I mean by that is that if someone on your team or someone in a position of authority were to say, "Wow, that really seems like a huge goal. Are you sure you can get this done?," it's tempting to say, "Oh, you might be right. I'm sorry. Let me think that through." The apology often comes from an unconscious desire to placate, or need to please, and reduce any possible tension.

But as you're owning the development and launch of a new offering, it's critical that you don't fall prey to this. As you lead teams and manage to a deadline, you need to stop the voice that may look to placate, and instead double down on your confidence. When you are questioned is exactly the moment to lean in to the work and assert that you can do it. It's okay if you want to double-check your assumptions, but don't apologize for the larger story you've shared. Instead, own it.

You can do this!

A Sample Press Release

As you're working to tell a bigger story, it's sometimes easy to get lost in the scale of the opportunity. As Jill helped explain, creating a press release (which you may or may not ever share) provides a simple set of constraints to think about the scale of the story you're describing, allowing you to think and talk "big" without risking credibility.

FOR IMMEDIATE RELEASE

Sept 1, 2020

Contact: sample@email.com

"Starboard Enterprises Launches Innovative Collaboration Tool for Business,

Lands Contracts with industry Leaders"

New York, NY

Starboard enterprise today announced the highly anticipated new offering designed to cure security loopholes for entire internet. The new offering allows easy access for customers to easily detect intruders on the website, and actually counters them with a new attack and report to authorities. "This is a critical disruption for an industry in need of a better solution to deal with the ever-increasing cyber security risks", said CEO Maria Paola.

Customers including Microsoft and Apple agree. "I'm thrilled to leverage Starboard's critical feature to combat the constant threats our customers are under, and protect the integrity of their data, "said Microsoft CTO, xxx. "In the new digital age, we need ore solutions like Starboard to deal with the threats we face. Added Apple CTO xxx.

The new solution is in a closed beta now, and will be available to all North American clients by Dec 2020.

About Starboard Enterprises: "Starboard Enterprises is a corporation based in New York, NY. Starboard is the world leader in security solutions for the digital age. For more equations about this release contact xxx.

Drafting a press release helps you think big.

By drafting this type of document, you will have set a framework of what success needs to look like by a certain date.

1. You can see in the first paragraph that the release describes what the offering is: It allows people to access it to detect intruders on their website and counters those

attackers. As you are developing your product, those become the core anchor items you need to remember.

2. It outlines the reason you did this.

3. It outlines the types of customers you hope to have.

4. It reminds you of what your business is, and its mission.

This format works whether you're tackling a cybersecurity issue or you plan to announce the grand opening of your local bakery. Include the business, why it exists, the product or service you're announcing, and who's excited to use it; that's it!

With this approach, you can tell yourself a bigger story, convey that story to your team or your investors, and set constraints to make it possible to deliver on in the process.

Chapter 8

It Really Is Okay to Make Mistakes

How to Plan for Them So You Can Quickly Recover

What you'll take away from this chapter:

In this chapter, we'll explore the ways in which you can use traditional tools like a financial model to think through what could go right and what could go wrong in your business. This analysis will help you build more confidence in your decision-making and empower you to more quickly recover from mistakes or missed opportunities.

The Others Arrive

Hannah and Sophie arrived bearing some small hostess gifts, which Jill graciously accepted.

"Hey, ladies—Maria and I were just going through her big vision of where Starboard is headed."

"Oh, cool!" Hannah couldn't wait to hear more about it.

"Hey, Maria!" Sophie glanced over Jill's shoulder to smile. "I'm sure Starboard is going to be the next Salesforce or something. And thanks again for meeting with me the other day! It was really helpful to talk things through with you."

"Any time!" Maria inhaled as she realized how glad she was to be part of this supportive group.

"Oh, I'm so glad you guys are all helping each other out! Well, come on in and have a seat. Can I grab you anything?" Jill gestured to Hannah and Sophie, encouraging them to get comfortable."

"Thanks, Jill, I'm all set." Hannah made her way to the seating area, debating in her mind if she was going to share what happened at work with the others.

"I'd love a water—I can grab it though." Sophie always felt awkward letting someone else get things for her.

"Don't be silly, I'll be right back with some drinks for everyone." Jill turned and walked briskly toward the kitchen.

Sophie made her way to the seats in the corner of the room, where Jill managed to keep some houseplants flourishing. Sophie was always amazed by how together Jill seemed to have things. Jill's kids were older, so she supposed that made things easier, but her house was not only neat and orderly, but nicely decorated with flourishing houseplants. Sophie pushed aside the contrasting thought of what she called "laundry mountain" looming in her basement.

"Hey, Sophie—so how is it going? Did you make any progress on your vision board or initial business plan?" Maria knew Sophie was juggling a full load with the kids.

"Yeah—I made progress on both, but I got a little overwhelmed once I got to the financial planning." Sophie grimaced as she thought about the five-year model she was working on in Excel.

"Well, it's not the most exciting thing to do!" Hannah's voice was dripping with sarcasm. "But do you mean you're struggling with the Excel? That's pretty straightforward. I can help you with that." Hannah had a significant amout of hands-on experience with Excel in her current role at work.

"No . . . while that's not my strong zone, I'm okay with the mechanics. It's the projecting into the future that's freaking me out. I can't guarantee what will happen in five years." Sophie had spent the last week working on parts of her business plan, but found herself completely stuck at that part.

"A little elaboration please," Maria chimed in, curious where the blocker was.

"Well, I am worried about being wrong. And I feel like I'm either making this crazy projection that no one will believe or I'm showing numbers that are too small to be exciting for investors."

"That's fair. I actually had the same type of feeling when I was trying to share the opportunity with investors." Maria had made some progress in that area with the press release, and understood what Sophie was anxious about.

Jill walked back in, placed a few drinks on the coffee table, and handed a water glass to Sophie.

"I completely understand the concerns you're having, but it's important to remember that this is a mental exercise before it's a mechanical one." Jill had experience running models for her large corporation and had seen her share of models for startups as well.

"What do you mean, Jill? I think I'm pretty savvy with Excel." Hannah hadn't heard those terms before.

"Well, using Excel is something in which it takes time to build formulas. But before you start doing that, which I call the mechanics, you need to really go through the mental exercise, using your imagination to make sense of it." Jill pulled a chair closer to the table, leaning in with the group.

"Okay, Maria, remember how we just went through putting together a press release? And the idea was to get really clear about the story you wanted someone else to tell about your business and how big it was?"

Maria nodded.

"Well, think of the financial model as your path to get there. It's sort of like looking at the GPS trip details all at once." Jill stood to go grab a piece of paper and a pen.

Jill drew a horizontal line with the words Year 1, Year 2, Year 3, Year 4, and Year 5 across the bottom.

"Let's start with the basics. Can you build out the assumptions of what you'll need to run your business today?"

"Jill, I think I missed some of the earlier conversations." Hannah felt a little out of her league in the conversation.

"Right—we've spent some time focusing on helping people understand where you are going. Assuming everything goes well, what the amazing, prosperous company you're building looks like."

"Now, we're drilling into how you show people the steps you'll take to get there." Jill drew an arrow to year 5.

"Oh, okay. I'm following." Hannah nodded. "When I run a project at work, I always get to the root of what we need to deliver, and then we walk back through our project plans for how we're going to get there. We use agile development, so obviously the 'how' changes as we go, but I'm able to build a high-level plan that allows us to properly budget and prioritize." Hannah felt more confident as she thought about the work she did every day.

"Exactly." Jill was glad to see Hannah relate her current experience to the exercise.

"Okay, so let's assume that in five years, you have a booming business with thousands of customers and millions in revenue. How did you get there?"

Jill circled year 1.

"For example, Maria, right now it's just you and a few freelancers you've been working with."

"Right." Maria nodded.

"Okay, let's say next year—year 2—you add more customers. What else could happen?" Jill asked rhetorically.

"Let's make some assumptions. You gain 100 customers and you now have to support those customers, so you'll need a support person. You also get feedback that allows you to build a new product offering for those customers, which you can charge them for. So you will also need more developers. Perhaps you'll hire a salesperson and a marketing person. You'll assume that the salesperson will sell x amount of your offering per year and that your marketing person will be able to generate a certain number of leads. All of these things are assumptions."

"Okay—but I think where I get stuck is feeling like I have to just tell people how I use what I have today," Sophie interjected. "Showing people how I keep adding and adding to get to bigger numbers somehow feels off."

"Right—but what you really need to do is stretch to imagine what you need every year to grow, including the increased costs associated with doing that. In fact, I would start with the total market opportunity as you understand it, and as Hannah said, walk back to how you got there." Jill glanced at Hannah reassuringly.

"So let's say you're planning to sell your solution to all Fortune 500 companies with large enterprise accounts by year 5. The numbers are about to get big, so get ready."

Jill pushed her pen to year 5. "Let's say that all Fortune 500 companies bought your solution at scale for $1,000,000. each. That's $500,000,000 in annual recurring revenue in year 5."

"Let's get back to year 1 to figure out how we get there. Perhaps in year 1 you just sell to some smaller companies at a lower price point, say $10,000 each. That success enables you to add new product features and hire more strategic sales reps. Then in turn by year 3 perhaps you've achieved 30% of your customers in the enterprise space, and you're able to build case studies that show other Fortune 500 companies how successful you've made them. This helps you get even more customers.

"As you map this out, you keep adding the additional costs it will take to get these types of customers, and ensure that they are happy with your solution."

"I get this, it makes sense. But I guess my fear is still that what if I'm wrong? What if I bake in all of these wins, but the customer doesn't come through?" Sophie figured she sounded a little pessimistic, but she didn't want to get it wrong.

"Then you can easily play with the model by looking at what happens to your income if, for example, those customers don't all buy the new product you made for them. What happens if the salesperson doesn't work out? What happens if the marketing person only creates half of the demand you were expecting?"

"That's exactly what made me freeze! What if I'm wrong about my assumptions, and therefore my whole model is wrong?"

"Your model won't be wrong, but your assumptions might be. That's what makes them assumptions." Jill decided to take another approach.

"Think of it this way: Let's say you were planning a trip."

"Okay . . ."

"You decide where you are going—let's say Boston."

"Then you get packed, get in your car, and drive there, using a map." Jill wrote the word Boston over Year 5 and wrote Indiana over Year 1, with a horizontal line between the two.

"Right . . ."

"Well, along the way, there might be traffic, there might be a detour, there might be a sudden storm, there might be an accident . . . you might be in an accident." Hannah smiled as Jill joked about this.

Jill then drew x's and stop signs and reroutes along the way.

"Right—"

"But those things wouldn't stop you from making the trip. You'll make the trip because that's where you are going, and you're confident that you'll figure out how to get there."

"It's the same with the financial projections. You know where you're going—to a wonderful amazing business with delighted customers. You're showing people the plan to get there, but there may be all sorts of hiccups along the way. Your model is basically showing people all the different ways you'll tackle those challenges and what could happen along the way."

"Like if traffic hits, you might arrive at 5 instead of 4."

"If your marketing hire doesn't produce, it might take you a year instead of six months to get the demand you need for your project."

"But that changes whether I get there in five years or not!" Sophie opened her hands as she spoke, reinforcing her point.

"Correct—if one of your assumptions is wrong, you may not get to that amazing business in five years. In fact, you may never get there. It's important to remember that plenty of businesses do fail. But the model allows you to work with all of the different assumptions and actually factor all of those scenarios in. You can actually use your concerns about failure to build a more robust model."

"That's a little intense." Hannah had a hard time imagining when she'd want to do this exercise, but Sophie actually found it calming.

"I think I get it. It's sort of like planning for the best possible outcome, and getting a chance to test out all of the different things that could happen along the way to get there." Sophie was thinking out loud.

"Exactly." Jill leaned back in her chair and smiled. "The model is your blueprint, and building your assumptions actually allows you to confront your fears, if you have them, head on! The financial model lets you see all of this with a click of a button, and make decisions accordingly. It's your perfect opportunity to forget about perfection, and actually model out mistakes!"

* * *

How to Get Started on the Financial Plan

The financial plan will become part of your living business plan, as well as a separate document that you'll regularly manage. Besides letting you know how your business is doing and showing how your business will grow over time, it also is critical in helping you ensure that you maintain enough cash to cover your expenses.

While you'll want to be able to easily see what can happen if things go extremely well, you'll also want to easily see what happens if you underestimate revenues.

Your financial plan will include your projected income statements, cash flow statements, and balance sheet. When you actually start to move your business forward, it will be important to sit down with a certified accountant to ensure that you're documenting everything correctly. The guidance offered in this chapter is not meant to be treated as accounting or legal advice. Rather, it is meant to help show you how to use accounting tools to better understand your own business. Again, please be sure to work with a trained accountant to file taxes and properly manage your books. It's also important to understand that different businesses offer different levels of consistency in financial planning. For example, a scalable business, which is covered here, is really a model showing how the business will scale with proper investment over time. If you are working on a nonprofit or consultancy, you may have more sporadic sales, and that's okay. The point of this exercise is simply to model out what is possible.

At a high level, some basic points to keep in mind are:

The income statement will show how much you project revenues, expenses, and profit (if any!) to be. Revenues are all the money you get from the sale of your products or services. Expenses are all the expenditures required to run your business, such as rent, labor, insurance, office supplies, and so on.

(Keep in mind that if you are selling software as a service (SaaS), for example, your revenue may not hit the books at the same time as your cash. For example, if you sell a solution that has a 12-month license, you'll recognize only 1/12th of the total annual amount you charged per month. Again—this is why an accountant is important!)

Your cash flow sheet will show your cash revenues and any payments for expenses; your balance sheet will show a summary of all the assets, current liabilities, and equity you have.

A breakeven analysis will show how much you need to sell before you will make a profit of any kind and stop "burning" cash.

You can do this!

Key Terms You Should Know

As you work to build out your models, it's important to keep a few terms in mind. There are countless terms and acronyms to keep track of as you work to chart your course. The following list covers some of the basic terms you'll be expected to include fluently in conversations, and you should know the triggers within your business.

- **CAC:** Customer acquisition cost (how much you paid to get that customer via ads/marketing, etc.)
- **LTV:** The lifetime value that customer has. This matters in justifying how much it cost you to get them.
- **COGs:** Cost of goods sold. This is how much it cost you to make the goods that you actually sold. Note that it's not part of how many items you have in inventory.
- **MRR:** Monthly recurring revenue (how much revenue you get for a customer per month).
- **ARR:** Annual recurring revenue (how much revenue you get for a customer in a year).
- **New Business:** Just what it sounds like. How much new business are you getting?
- **Expansion Business:** For a given customer, how much expansion business do you have? Are they buying additional licenses of your current product? Are they buying new solutions you're selling to them on top of their initial product?
- **Churn:** What percentage of your customers drop off, meaning what percentage of your customers stop purchasing your product in the future? If, for example, you obtain 1,000 new customers but 90% of them don't renew their subscription for your solution, you have a very high churn rate. That's not good. If you obtain 1,000 new customers but only 2% of them don't renew their subscription for your solution, then you have a very low churn rate. That is very good!

Developing a Set of Assumptions for Your Model

A financial model is a five-year forecast that shows your projected income statement, cash flow statement, and balance sheet. While you can't easily predict exactly what will happen because you are creating a new business, you can build a list of assumptions that will help describe your path.

Before you start to input numbers into a financial tool, first list the assumptions you are making about your business. Some assumptions to consider could include:

- The number of employees you plan to add over time and each of their projected salaries
- The amount you plan to charge for your product or service
- The amount of revenue a salesperson can generate (ie: how many products or services will she sell per month?)
- The percentage growth you expect per year
- The amount of revenue an inside salesperson can generate
- The number of new customers you can gain per month
- The number of services or products those new customers will purchase
- The amount of support those customers need
- The amount of travel you need to conduct
- The cost of a good sold
- The cost to gain a customer through advertising

Your initial assumption list will be quite long, but the idea is to start really thinking through all the factors that can contribute to your success. It's sometimes tempting to simply document that you'll hire x number of people and generate y amount of revenue. But to make this an effective exercise, you should consider all the factors that contribute to your success or failure. Once you have all of those, you can start to develop a model that allows you to easily see projections of your future business.

Chapter 9

You Don't Have to Wait for Revenue to Ask for Funding

Create a Compelling Pitch Deck That Gets Others on Board

What you'll take away from this chapter:

In this chapter, we'll explore the ways in which you can succinctly describe what you are working on with a solid pitch deck. You'll also find helpful resources on multiple funding options, ranging from nondilutive to traditional investments.

Six Months Later ...

"Sophie, I really need to pay you a compliment." Jill was being earnest. She, Maria, Sophie, and Hannah were taking a walk together through the streets of the small community.

"I'm really impressed with the way you've bootstrapped your company so far. You've got two months of traction with some really impressive customers. From the outside looking in, it's hard to believe you've only been doing this in your spare time with limited resources."

"Yeah, Sophie, it's pretty amazing. Do you think you're going to raise capital now, or are you going to bootstrap a little longer?" Maria was curious. With Jill's help Maria had been able to raise a small angel investment round, and was rooting for Sophie's business to succeed as well.

"I'm not sure if I'm going to raise capital or if I'm going to try to build this more slowly and organically, as a consultative business." Sophie had built her model with multiple assumptions, and knew if she raised capital she could do more faster, but she had also been focused enough on generating cash that she hadn't spent any time thinking about her pitch to investors.

"Well, honestly, venture capital is expensive. If you can figure out how to really build your business without it, in many ways you'd be better off, but I know getting funding has really empowered me to move more quickly and get the right people on board to help out." Maria slowed her pace as she thought about her investment win over the last month. After getting her investor pitch together and maximizing the connections she had made, she had been able to obtain two term sheets from prospective investors and negotiated fairly competitive terms.

"Yeah, one of the things I've been excited to learn in the last few months is how much nondilutive funding is out there too. And this business is just starting to feel like a third child." Sophie was making a joke (sort of).

"It really depends on the business you're trying to build. If you're working on that hockey stick plan with quickly accelerating growth, you'll probably need outside funding at some point to move forward. If you're able to generate an additional income on your own terms without it, and achieve your primary mission, I wouldn't bother."

"Right, but at the same time, sometimes the best things happen with constraints in the beginning. I know we have projects at work that have literally blown through millions of dollars and produced nothing because they are bloated, people-heavy things. While I managed a project that came in at budget and was deemed a success last year, I can tell you we spent *a lo*t on things I would not have paid for myself." Hannah smirked as she thought of the countless dollars they had been asked to budget for an outside contractor.

"Well, Sophie, if you don't need the money, then don't raise it. I know I wish I had raised a little more wisely, a little earlier on. I had a full year of traction with some awesome customers before I felt comfortable asking for investment, because I wanted to prove myself." Maria thought of the countless sleepless nights she had had, managing customers while also working on her day job.

"But I look back and think I could have started to raise capital when I had about two or three months of strong customer traction."

"Well, if you're up for it, I'd love to show you where I'm at, and what I'm thinking, and take a look at whatever pitch deck you used to raise," Sophie suggested.

"Of course, and I think it's also worth digging in to other nondilutive funding options that might also be out there. I didn't really explore a ton of those, and if you can find nondilutive funding, you can avoid giving up a large percentage of your company."

"I think the key to whether you decide to fundraise or not is that you realize that the most effective entrepreneurs are resourceful," Jill said wisely. "In addition to many successes, you'll likely have lean periods or months when things aren't going well. You need to be resourceful to deal with any challenge that comes your way and handle constraints. Moreover, each time you raise, you should consider that you may need to raise again, and that the current round is really for about 18 months of runway, of which you'll spend three to six months working to raise again."

"That makes sense. I feel like I'm actually pretty resourceful already." Sophie was thinking out loud. "I'd love to take a look at what you used to raise, though, Maria."

"Sure thing!"

When they got back to Jill's house, Maria pulled up a PowerPoint slide deck. It was beautifully designed and professional looking. "So on the first slide, I just put my company logo." Maria flipped to the second slide. "Then I outlined the massive industry problem. In our case it was the security vulnerability in the market." Maria flipped again. "The next slide outlines how we can solve this massive problem." From there, she flipped to show her remaining slides, which covered a brief demo, her approach to the business model, the total market size, why her company was different, key milestones her company has delivered on, her team with bios, and general financials.

Sophie read through it, realizing that although it wasn't a ton of information—it was just a handful of slides—the way in which the slides were presented and the attention to detail required were pretty significant and impressive.

Maria watched Sophie processing the information.

"Sometimes being succinct is harder than writing in details about what you're building. I know this looks simple, but I also think it will take me some time to do it right."

"Sophie, you don't have to raise right now ... but *I know you can do this.*"

* * *

When Bootstrapping ...

The technical definition of bootstrapping is using your own existing resources to get into or out of a situation. In this case, Sophie had been working to develop her business and obtain customers without looking for or accepting any outside capital. If you can self-fund your own business, you will own 100% of it. This is critical to understand because in the tech community, stories are so often told of companies successfully raising capital that it becomes easy to think that the act of raising was the win. But for the entrepreneur, it's the creation of value that is the win. Whether you continue to build your business toward profitability or ultimately sell your business, the more of it you own, the more capital you'll keep personally.

From personal experience, I know that if I had figured out how to get as far as I did in my business without any outside capital or at the very least with more nondilutive capital, I would have personally increased my wealth more. I know of other entrepreneurs who raised less than I did but personally gained more.

If you are working on bootstrapping your business, there are a number of sources that can be helpful to you.

Crowdfunding

If you would like to test out the market excitement for your offering, and you would like to gain the funding necessary to build or make it, you can attempt crowdfunding. There are a number of online solutions for this, with Kickstarter and Indiegogo being two of the most well known right now.

The idea of creating a crowdfunding campaign using a solution like Kickstarter, is that you will set an amount you are trying to raise in order to build your solution. If you don't raise enough, your campaign has failed, and you are under no obligation to build. If your campaign meets or exceeds the number you set, then you will receive the funds, but you also need to make sure you can deliver on your promise.

I have now accepted multiple companies into the Techstars accelerator that had previously completed successful Kickstarters. Their track records demonstrated that they were able to generate consumer interest in their offerings, and their ability to deliver on their promises provided a glimpse into the commitment that they would have to their companies and to their customers.

If you consider launching a Kickstarter or other crowdfunding site, it's important to build a basic website that skillfully explains your offering. Tools like WIX or SquareSpace make it simple for nontechnical founders to easily build a website, and set up basic marketing features like SEO (search Engine optimization), social media integration, and stock email campaigns. You can also create beta stage logos and graphics using tools like Adobe Spark, which comes with a variety of preformatted, well-designed options.

Government

There are also a number of resources available to entrepreneurs via the government. You can visit https://grants.gov to learn more about federally backed grant options for new businesses. While highly competitive, they are worth exploring.

In addition, the Small Business Innovation Research (SBIR) program is a federal initiative designed to drive small businesses to participate in federal research and development. Although obtaining funding is highly competitive, the program is designed to empower businesses to profit from the commercialization of their offerings while infusing the government with more entrepreneurial initiative. What's important for female entrepreneurs to know is that one of the core missions of the initiative is to "foster and encourage participation in innovation and entrepreneurship by women, and socially or economically disadvantaged persons." By law, U.S. government agencies with budgets exceeding $100 million have to allocate at least 3.2% to SBIR. As stated on the SBIR website, those agencies include the Department of Agriculture, the Department of Commerce, the Department of Defense, the Department of Education, the Department of Energy, the Department of Health and Human

Services, the Department of Homeland Security, the Department of Transportation, the Environmental Protection Agency, the National Aeronautics and Space Administration, and the National Science Foundation.

While each department provides their own requests for proposals, it's helpful to know that there are three main phases, as outlined on the SBIR site. If you're awarded a Phase I grant, you'll typically receive $150,000 or less and use the funds to establish the merit of your technical work. If you're awarded a Phase II award, you could receive approximately $1,000,000 to build on what you did in Phase I. And in Phase III you could be working to pursue commercialization of your work.

Historically, the SBIR program has been difficult to navigate and many departments still are, but Warren Katz, a successful entrepreneur, investor, mentor, and managing director with Techstars, has spent a significant amount of time and energy working with the Air Force to streamline the process to make it easier for others to apply for grants. In fact, many of the companies who participate in the accelerator he runs end up funding their companies primarily with nondilutive funds. I think with the new streamlined process it's worth doing research in the areas as a means to understand all your options.

Private Grants

Many philanthropic organizations provide grants in areas of strategic interest. You can perform a basic search to try to discover them. You'll quickly see pages of options, although many grants are limited in the total amount they provide to less than $20,000. However, another method to consider is leveraging grants to help your customers pay for your product. This generates actual revenue for your company and is helpful to your customers.

You can start by looking at more established companies in your vertical market. Large organizations will often help customers pay for their solutions by helping them find and complete proposals for grant funding. Often you'll see the list of funding sources on their websites as a tool for customers to buy their solutions. You can use the same information to make contact with those organizations and research potential options for your business and your customers.

Seeking Investors

Each time you accept outside investment, you are giving up a percentage of your company in the form of equity. With this exchange you also give up some control and, depending on the deal terms that you received, in the event of a liquidity event your investor may be paid first—before you are as the founder. However, there are many times that taking investment is the right thing to do. You can move faster, get ahead of your competition, and you may simply need it to build the business you have conceptualized.

If you decide to go this route, it's important to understand the terms at play, as they can wildly impact the amount of ownership you may be giving up under a varying set of circumstances. For example, an investor may set a liquidation preference of 2□. This could mean that if the company was acquired, your investor would get 2□ their initial investment, before you receive anything. While the original agreement may have set your ownership at 50%, if you sold for $4 million and they had invested $2 million but set that type of liquidation preference, you would get nothing at the time the deal closed because $2 \times \$2M$ is $4M). That said, under those terms, if you sold your company for $40 million, if they exercised their liquidation preference, they would still get $4 million, but you'd get 50% of the remaining $16 million. All of these terms are designed to help the investor optimize their return and to incentivize the entrepreneur to build the business as big as possible. But it's critical to know what you're getting in to.

You can learn more about how venture investment works and the various terms you need to be aware of in Brad Feld's book *Venture Deals*.

If you do decide to seek outside capital or investment, you should first do research on the type of investors in your vertical market or industry and the stage of companies in which they invest. For example, if you are building a company with AI capabilities, research investors who have played in that space, and also research the other companies in which they invested. Research the location of the investors, and understand that many will want to invest in companies in their geographic location. There are several online tools available to help you research this such as Crunchbase and Pitchbook.

Seek out local events to network with potential investors, and if you end up in a meeting, ask good questions.

Don't go approach an investor and simply ask them to invest. Ask questions that convey your understanding of their history and demonstrate your desire to generate returns with a company that can scale. There's a statement that's been made a thousand times, which is "if you want investment, ask for advice. If you want advice, ask for investment"—which really means that if you're just asking for money, you're not describing the value you're creating and you're not demonstrating any curiosity about the investor's business. Neither of these makes an investor interested in funding your business. But they may offer advice on what you could do instead.

If you ask smart questions that demonstrate that you understand your market, and your customers and their investment thesis, they might turn around and start talking to you about investment. One of my first investor meetings that actually went well started with a question I asked in a Q&A session following an investor panel presentation. I had just finished negotiating a contract and had had an early conversation with another company that had alluded to partnering or acquiring. So I asked the panel, "How do you recommend that entrepreneurs handle partnership conversations that allude to acquisitions when they are still very early in the company lifecycle development?" This question got the investor's attention and led to additional meetings, and ultimately a term sheet. It's important to note that I didn't make anything up to try to sound smarter or better off than I was. But I took the time to ask something that was real and that I thought might be of interest to an investor.

Angel and Venture Investment

Angel investors are typically high-net-worth individuals who may invest independently in a company, or they may pool their money with other angels to invest a larger amount in a company. A venture investor is a person who invests a fund's money into a company. Both angel investors and venture investors are looking for large returns when they invest in your company. When you are working to fundraise for your business, you'll use your deck to pitch the investor. It may take many meetings before you find an investor willing to put money into your company, since they are often looking for very high returns and therefore are often assuming high risks. In fact, approximately 1% of companies that seek some sort of investment receive it. Assuming you do find an investor that is impressed with your company and solution, he or she will share a term sheet. The term sheet is a document that outlines the terms of the deal: how much money the investor will put in and how much ownership of the company they will assume. After you negotiate the terms of the term sheet, you will enter a phase of due diligence. At this point you will be asked for everything from your security process to your customer lists. Assuming that process goes smoothly, you will receive the final deal documents and the funding as originally specified. Throughout the deal process, it's critical to work with a lawyer who understands venture terms.

You'll need to be sure that you understand common valuations of businesses at your stage and size, as well as basic venture terms.

* * *

In summary, the best advice I've been given is that sales solve everything. If you can sell your solution and deliver real value to a customer, you can focus more on that and less on raising capital. However, if you need capital to get your product to market or to continue to expand your market, you have many options available, ranging from private venture funding to public grants to crowdsourcing. Regardless of the avenue, or multiple avenues, you take, it will be critical to understand the competitive landscape you are in, and to put your best foot forward. The resources in this chapter are designed to help.

You can do this!

More on the Sample Pitch Deck for Investors

Over the years, I've built several decks independently for my startup as well as for board buy-in in a large corporation. I've also reviewed multiple decks at pitch competitions and for investment review. If you do a basic search online, you'll find no shortage of different approaches to take. Even within Techstars, we rely on a few different templates, with Alex Iskold, the former managing director for Techstars New York, writing a very instructive blog post on the topic, which you can find at https://alexiskold.net/2015/12/31/the-perfect-investor-deck-for-seed-round/.

At its core, the goal of the pitch deck is to succinctly describe the value your business is creating. The following visual helps to describe the key foundational pieces.

Key Elements of Your Pitch Deck

Place each of these elements on a separate slide using a tool like Microsoft PowerPoint or Google Slides. You can experiment with the order, just make sure it's logical

1. The gorgeous company logo you made.	2. The massive problem (opportunity) you've found.	3. Your unique, amazing solution to the problem (opportunity)	4. What you've managed to do about all of this! (your traction)
5. Why you're so amazing! How your solution or I.P. separates you from the masses.	6. How you make all the money! (your business model)	7. The size of the market you're going after. (hint: bigger is better)	8. Professional pictures and bios of you and your amazing team.
9. What you need to make this all happen and a nice timeline view.			

What to Include in Your Pitch Deck

A Little About Accelerators

Over the past 10 years, multiple accelerators and incubators have emerged, all designed to help companies work through their investment needs, and many of which also provide some initial funding. While I currently work as a managing director for Techstars, there are multiple programs that could be beneficial to you as you work to source your initial round of funding. That said, Techstars is recognized as a leader in the space and currently runs 50 accelerators around the world, with a global network of investors and mentors available to help move your business along faster.

If you are looking to move your business along faster, an accelerator is designed to accept a limited number of companies, provide some initial investment, and help accelerate the growth of your company. At Techstars, accepted companies receive up to $120,000 in funding, along with access to over $1 million in resources. Of the 1,600-plus companies that have gone through the program, over 85% are active or have been acquired, and huge success stories include those such as PillPack, which was acquired by Amazon in 2018 for $1 billion, and Send Grid, which had an IPO. Other examples of accelerator programs include YCombinator and 500Startups.

Incubators are designed to help early-stage entrepreneurs explore different business models, incubating their business. Many universities and community colleges, ranging from Harvard and MIT to Ivy Tech Community College, offer business incubators to students to help develop their ideas and consider the next step in their entrepreneurial journey. Further, organizations including the National Association for Community College Entrepreneurship (NACCE) have emerged to help foster entrepreneurship and provide resources for those in community colleges. If you are early in your journey, it's worth exploring what resources may be available to you in your local community.

Some Key Terms to Know

The following are just a few key terms to understand as you're raising capital. You can learn much more about the venture terms by reading *Venture Deals*.

Key Term	Meaning
Valuation	The perceived value of your business today based on future value and traction to date. Like in real estate, the market of the day will impact your valuation. So try to do some research on companies of similar stages and sizes.
Pre-money valuation	The value of your company before you accept any capital investment.
Post-money valuation	The new valuation of your business with the additional funding. For example, if you were valued at $1 million and raised $1 million, your post-money valuation is $2 million.

Key Term	Meaning
Liquidation preference	In the event your company has a liquidity event (is acquired, for example) the preference the investor can take. For example, if it's a 1☐ liquidation preference and the investor put in $1 million, the most they would get in the event of a liquidity event would be either their ownership or their liquidation preference, which in this case would be 1☐ $1, or $1 million. If there was a 2☐ liquidation preference, they would get 2☐ $1 million, or $2 million, or the higher amount of their ownership.

Additional Reading from Techstars and Other Ideas

1. *Do More Faster: Techstars Lessons to Accelerate Your Startup* by David Cohen and Brad Feld
2. *Venture Deals: Be Smarter Than Your Lawyer and Venture Capitalist* by Brad Feld and Jason Mendelson
3. Research investors and funds that focus on inclusion including but not limited to:
   - Backstage Capital
   - Golden Seeds
   - Harlem Capital
   - Valor
   - Springboard
   - Female Founders Fund
   - Intel Capital and Diversity Fund
   - Tory Burch Foundation
   - 37Angels
   - Pivotal Ventures

Your Data Room

As you make your way through an investment process, you'll want to make sure that all of the documents relevant to your company are in one secure, easily accessible place. The following provides a quick snapshot of some of the file types you should be prepared to show if asked. It's much easier to organize this type of file system before you're in the due diligence process so you don't waste any time searching for relevant documentation when the time comes.

You will need folders for:

1. Company formation documents
2. Stock ownership agreements, your capitalization table
3. All employee files and records, including IP assignments, roles, job descriptions, and so on
4. Customers
5. Tax/accounting
6. Legal/intellectual property, patents, and so on
7. Any material liabilities, lawsuits, product defects, and so on
8. Security for your products and your internal procedures, and product details
9. Sales and marketing collateral and pipeline reporting
10. Software code and any open-source libraries

The following is a visual of what your data room might look like.

Create Your Data Room for Due Diligence

Company formation documents, right to do business	Stock/ownership agreements/cap table	All employee files (IP assignments, employment agreements, contract info, roles)	Customers, contracts, terms, locations

Tax/accounting details	Legal docs/intellectual property/patents lawsuits	Security/internal and product details	Sales prospects/pipeline	Software code/any open licenses used

A Data Room for Your Documents

Section III

Lead and Operationalize

Good leaders organize and align people around what the team needs to do....

Great leaders motivate and inspire people with why they're doing it.

—Marilyn Hewson, CEO, Lockheed Martin

Chapter 10

Empathy Is One of Your Biggest Assets

Use It to Understand Your Customers and Make Your Teams Stronger

What you'll take away from this chapter:

In this chapter, we'll explore the ways in which you can leverage your high EQ to build customer personas, continue to develop and improve your product, and make your teams work more effectively together.

As Starboard Grew

With Jill's coaching, Maria was able to update her company documentation and tell a better story to investors. In addition, the work she had done empowered her to gain clarity on her business and gain additional traction in the market, completing initial software development and landing key customers. She had leveraged that momentum and, after several investor pitches, she was able to secure a modest amount of funding, or a seed round, for her company, which enabled her to scale more quickly.

In just one year post-funding, Maria's business was growing at an incredible pace. She'd hired multiple people, including Hannah, who not only led multiple development projects but also served as a key customer support contact. Hannah was convinced that at some point she would probably start her own business, but joining Maria's team as an early hire enabled her to see how a startup could work and build her leadership muscle across multiple domains. Starboard had sold her initial software solution to multiple medium-sized businesses and were preparing to scale into enterprise accounts (accounts for large customers where the average order size may be significantly more because there are significantly more licensed users for the account).

Jill now served as a formal member of Maria's advisory board and stopped by the office, which was in a small office space downtown, about once a month.

With her bobbed brown hair tucked neatly behind her ears, Jill straightened her collar before entering the office. Maria had worked hard to make it feel like an inclusive environment for the 20 employees now working there. While still a modest space, there was a small waiting area with a few chairs and a table, along with coffee, water, and a small Lego table for visiting children. The office abounded with natural light, and there were open desks throughout the center, with a few strategically placed areas for private conversations. There was a small kitchen with plenty of sparkling waters and healthy snacks for employees. There was also a room with yoga mats for employees who wanted to take a break to meditate or stretch. The gender-neutral restrooms were stocked with feminine products, mouthwash, and holistic hand creams and soaps.

One of the newer hires, Christine, greeted Jill as she walked in. "Would you like me to show you to Maria's office?" Christine was a recent college grad who Maria had hired to handle event planning and logistics.

"Thanks—you're Christine, right?"

"Um, yes." Christine smiled, surprised but thrilled that Jill remembered her. "It's not a big place, but it's right down this hallway."

"Maria, Jill is here."

Maria glanced up from her computer, and walked over to greet Jill.

"Thanks, Christine. Jill, thank you for coming over."

"Of course, how are things going? It looks wonderful in here."

"Thank you. It's going really well. I mean, we're gaining new customers every week, and things are in line with that plan I created."

"Fantastic."

"But I'm also starting to field so many support calls now, and I don't have as much time to give to each person the way

I did before." Maria sometimes felt that things were unraveling beyond her control, and wasn't sure how to keep things running smoothly all of the time.

"Well, that's actually a good problem to have. If no one's complaining, they aren't actually using your software."

"Fair!" Maria smiled as she thought of all the people actively using her solution.

"I think this is an opportunity for you to really start to scale your team and think about how to use your compassion and empathy as a way to build better results for the business."

"What do you mean?"

"Well, if you can standardize the quality of care you put into each relationship, you can use the feedback to improve your product development and increase sales through those follow-on deals we talked about."

"I'm not sure what you mean. How do I standardize the quality of care?" Maria asked.

"I mean, 1 on 1 you're working closely with everyone, and your deep-dive into your customer's needs early on is what led to your success. But now you have to figure out how to standardize that behavior, so it's a norm across the organization."

"Oh … okay." Maria was following.

"You already have Hannah here, right, leveraging her experience in delivering projects on time, to make sure development is going well, coupled with your strong product vision. And you have a full-time software development lead now, too, right?"

"Of course!" Maria knew she had built the foundation for a strong team.

"Well, I'd do an all-hands meeting every week while you're still small, to go over the support needs, the sales questions people are getting, and the development needs. You can also use that to enhance your product."

"That's a good point. I've been doing an all-hands meeting, but more to report to everyone on what's happening across groups—not to have them share the product cycle." Maria realized that although she was having large meetings, they more or less had served as vehicles for top-down communications.

"Right—I know you're doing agile development with your software team, but consider bringing the customer support and salespeople into the loop to make sure you're really getting all the needs understood.

"You are already empathizing with the customer. You want to build that into your corporate culture so everyone else here does, too." Jill knew that in the digital age, customer experience was king. Maria had naturally understood and developed user personas to figure out what product features to deliver. Now she needed to translate that understanding to the entire company so people knew how to market, sell, and support based on the individual customer profile.

"That will make your teams stronger, your customers happier, and ultimately your company more successful."

"But isn't there a slight concern that I'd be wasting people's time? Is pulling a salesperson or support person off the phone to meet with the whole group just potentially reducing their impact?" Maria really wanted to get this right.

"I can see why you think that, but I think you'll see that by connecting the dots among your teams, you'll actually make everyone more efficient. Making sure that the engineers really understand the challenges that the customer support person faces will enable them to approach problems differently. Likewise, as salespeople learn about what's already being worked on in real time, they can be more strategic as they talk to customers about features and when they'll really be available."

"Oh, that makes sense."

"Right—and when people feel known, they feel safe. And when people feel safe they learn better. It's rooted in science, and will actually make your overall company more productive." This was one of Jill's favorite stats she'd learned while researching how people learn and the importance of psychological safety for creativity.

"Super interesting, Jill—so if I bring people together to share their experiences, we'll actually have a higher-performing, more empathetic team ... "

"Exactly."

Creating an Environment Where People Want to Work Starts with Knowing People

Studies show that across the general population, EQ (emotional intelligence) and levels of empathy are likely statistically equal among men and women. Researchers Peter Salovey and John Mayer originally defined emotional intelligence as "the ability to monitor one's own and other people's emotions, to discriminate between different emotions and label them appropriately, and to use emotional information to guide thinking and behavior." Their studies showed that if you develop and leverage your emotional intelligence, you can have better interpersonal relationships because you have better self-perceptions and awareness. You may also be perceived more positively by others, have an easier time negotiating, improved self-esteem, and make better decisions combining rationale or logic with emotion rather than being responsive.

While studies show that men and women are just as likely to have high EQs, women who make it into leadership positions often have higher EQs than men who did. That's likely because EQ is needed to navigate a landscape that isn't biased toward women, but rather against them. If, like Maria, you managed to receive investment and get your business off the ground, there is a pretty good likelihood that you have a strong EQ. As a leader of a growing organization, this will be critical in managing your teams and your board of directors.

Understanding the implicit motivations of others and relating to their experiences makes it easier to navigate team dynamics, understand positioning within a board, and ensure that you are supporting your customers in an effective way that will make them more likely to renew. This ability to relate also allows you to more easily incorporate customer needs into your product roadmap.

But this doesn't mean that you must rely only on your intrinsic interpretation of a situation to make improvements. In fact, that's not really scalable as your business grows and your time is crunched.

Understanding Your Employees' Working Styles

HR leaders often leverage various personality tests to better understand team dynamics and make suggestions to improve communications, which in turn an improve overall team performance.

It's critical to ensure that you comply with best practices and guidelines if you are deploying a test to employees. Most tests require administration by a trained or certified professional. Some to consider include the DISC assessment, which is designed to let you know how people work and react. Another is the Myers-Briggs, which helps you understand people's basic tendencies. With either approach, some key things to consider is what gives someone energy and what depletes them.

The point of asking employees to take these types of tests is not so that you can personally judge them. The point is to make sure you uncover their natural or preferred working styles so that you can empower your teams for success. If you know you have several introverts in your company who are, by definition, energized by being alone and depleted by being in group settings, you might consider creating more quiet spaces for them.

If you have several extroverts in your team, by definition, you know they are more energized by being in groups, and their energy is depleted when they are alone too long. So in that case, you would want to create more opportunities for group engagement.

Little Things Lead to Bigger Success

At a high level your objective is to create an environment where people *want* to work.

In addition, although you are working to create the environment that yields the best results for the company, it's important to be tuned in to what makes people likely to succeed or not. For example, sometimes in an attempt to be "nice," employees will tell a co-worker struggling with being able to attend a meeting to "just not worry about it." But in reality their efforts to be kind might result in making that person feel excluded, and as if their work doesn't matter. Try not to schedule meetings for times when you know key leaders or rising leaders can't attend. Aim for important meetings in the middle of the day. Many organizations have emerged that focus on best practices in inclusion. One example is MOR (https://morismore.com/), a consulting firm focused on helping companies navigate inclusion opportunities.

You'll also recall that Jill made a point of saying Christine's name. When people hear their names, they automatically feel safer. It's part of our tribal roots. When we are known we are safe, and if we are safe we can learn and be creative. Teachers know to greet each student by name at the start of the school day, because students who feel safe learn more easily. Likewise, if your employees feel that you know them, and you can call them by their names, they will feel safer and be more able to perform.

Working Together to Improve Outcomes and Customer Satisfaction

In the narrative for this chapter, Jill and Maria also discussed the importance of cross-collaboration among teams. Collaboration among diverse groups actually leads to more efficient outcomes, as well as an increase in innovation. As you work to build your teams with specific functions like sales, engineering, and customer service, don't lose sight of what you used to manage when you were first starting your company. In the early days, you, as the founder, likely handled first sales, first customer support inquiries, and may have built the first product.

Feedback and understanding from each division yields better results for everyone. If your customer support team continuously reports on a similar bug or customer challenge, one of your engineers may quickly realize that it relates to a new feature they recently pushed out in the code. Likewise, if a salesperson gains a clear view into the long-term product roadmap, she can more easily articulate that vision to customers to build long-term meaningful relationships.

These are just a few examples of where an increased focus on cross-collaboration and empathy among team members and for customers can lead. So while the term "empathy" is sometimes used in a subversive way to imply that those who possess it are somehow more emotional or prone to irrational decision-making, I'm confident that an emphasis on empathy can lead to a better customer experience and stronger, healthier team dynamics.

You can do this!

Resources to Help You Navigate Employees

Administering a personality test to your employees can help you better understand team dynamics and improve communications, which can improve overall team performance.

Table 10.1   Personality Assessments for Employees

Test	What It Shows	Where to Find It	Requires a Pro?
DISC	People's dominant behaviors at work based on four different personality traits: D (Dominance) I (Influence) S (Steadiness) C (Conscientiousness)	https://www.discprofile.com/what-is-disc/overview/	Yes
Myers-Briggs	Based on Carl Jung's research, the premise is that many traits that appear random are actually orderly, based on how people perceive or judge situations	https://www.myersbriggs.org/my-mbti-personality-type/mbti-basics/home.htm?bhcp=1	Yes

Developing Customer Personas

As you work to better understand your customer, developing a customer persona chart will help you as you work to support them, market to them, and ultimately build products for them. To get started, define each of the types of customers you have. Think about what matters to them, what happens in their day, and how your software or solution impacts them. Are you making their lives easier or harder? How could you improve?

Table 10.2   Define Customer Profiles or Personas

Customer Persona Examples	Why They Are Using Your Solution	What Matters to Them
Student	They are required to.	Ease of use
Teacher	Your solution makes it easier to grade or assess their students.	Ease of use and accuracy of reporting or measurement
Administrator	Your solution makes it easier to monitor schoolwide activity.	Analytics and reporting on performance holistically

Mapping the Customer Experience

As you consider how you market, support, sell to, or engage with your customer, you can map out their experience throughout the whole day and where your solution comes into play. How much time do they spend in your solution? What other tools do they use at the same time? How easy or hard is it to navigate among them? Are there any offline activities that they have to complete as well? When they require support from your company, who do they speak with or engage with? How many steps do they need to take to get the help they need? Do other people similar to their profile have the same experience? Is there anything a salesperson should be aware of if she is trying to sell more solutions to the customer? Have you been making each persona in the account happy? Are there any challenges to be aware of?

There are countless questions you can ask about the customer experience. The more you understand, the more you and your teams can empathize with the customer. When you empathize with the customer, you develop stronger marketing materials that speak to their unique challenges, you provide better support because you feel their pain and want to resolve it, and you ultimately will sell them more solutions because they will trust that your service works and has their goals in mind.

Chapter 11

Instill a Growth Mindset in Your Teams

Constant Change and Transitions Are Never Easy

What you'll take away from this chapter:

In this chapter, we'll explore the ways in which you must be prepared for constant change. As George Bernard Shaw famously said, "Those who can't change their minds can't change anything." That statement has never been more true. With the constant threat of disruption, the rise of artificial intelligence, and the shift in foreign policies, companies need to be constantly prepared for change. In this chapter, you'll learn about the importance of instilling a growth mindset to handle change, get more comfortable pivoting, and continuing to innovate.

When You Move Beyond the Startup and People Start to Silo into Positions

"Someone actually just said ... that's not my job!" Hannah had positioned her hands on her hips, and looked at Maria, exasperated.

"Seriously? What did you tell them?" Maria raised her eyebrows. That wasn't a sentence she had expected to hear at her company.

"I asked her what she thought her job was." Hannah crossed her arms, recalling how incredulous she had felt responding to the statement.

"And ... ?" Maria wanted to hear more.

"She said, 'My job was described to me as sending emails to prospective clients and helping customers troubleshoot challenges over the phone.'" Hannah relayed with the same flat tone the employee had used.

"What did you *ask* her to do?" Maria wondered what could have prompted this type of exchange.

"I asked her to put together a report showing a master view of customer calls, and the types of issues they were having, so we could use it to better inform our development."

"Well, that's a perfectly reasonable extension of her work."

"Right—if I were her I would have jumped on it, to show the additional strategic value I could provide." Hannah still couldn't believe it.

"Please explain to her that we expect everyone at this company to have a growth mindset. New tasks will come up, new objectives will be created, and we expect our employees to be able to pivot and adjust so that we as an organization can be prepared to pivot and adjust."

"I hear you—believe me. I'll talk to her privately about this. She may just not be a good fit for the organization, but I think it may be worth doing a larger workshop for the entire team. I don't want one attitude to infect everyone else's." Hannah thought that this was a potentially larger cultural issue for the company than Maria was articulating.

"That's a fair point." Maria was still trying to process the story as Hannah walked out. She had always sought to do her best at every job and achieve more on top of what she was asked. She assumed that one should always be learning, which is partly how she ended up starting a company. As they were starting to hire more people, she was surprised that someone came on board with that type of attitude. She thought this might be a good conversation to have with Jill, who was really serving as an executive coach at this point.

"Maria—Hannah is right. You need to make this a bigger part of your culture." Jill's voice was actually stern. She had made the trip over again after hearing the genuine concern in Maria's voice when she called.

"You can't bring on people who think they are there to just perform a task like scooping ice cream. You need to instill your core values and mission into the team, so that they continue to learn and build based on shared values and a common mission. As Carol

Dweck pointed out in her book *Mindset: The New Psychology of Success*, you need to create an organizational growth mindset."

"Right—I guess I need to develop a growth leadership mindset to push this forward." Maria started to think about how her own attitudes may have led to some of the behaviors she was seeing.

"Exactly. You know, there's a great quote from Antoine de Saint-Exupéry, the author of *The Little Prince*, on this one: "If you want to build a ship, don't drum up people to collect wood and don't assign them tasks and work, but rather teach them to long for the endless immensity of the sea."

"Right, I've heard that one ... I think they use it at Netflix to keep people motivated." Maria got the concept, but just putting feel-good quotes out to the team somehow didn't seem to completely fit the bill for what was needed.

"Maria, this comes naturally to you, but you've got a new thing to learn—how to instill the same growth mindset in your teams that you hold yourself. You don't want people in here working on a specific thing for a specific project that is assigned to them. You can't assume that just because you care deeply about this, everyone else here does, too. That's how people will leave this place, eager to go home to something they care more deeply about. You want people to share and buy into the mission of Starboard ... When they do that, they'll do whatever it is that needs to be done to get there."

"So this really is on me. I'm going to give this some thought." Maria thought about the mental energy she used to spend on leaving her own job, And now here she was with her own company and its unique mission.

So Maria started brainstorming on how she could instill this type of aspirational focus and mindset into her teams ... She knew she could do it.

* * *

Building for Organizational Success through Your Company's Mission

The exchanges described among Hannah, Maria, and Jill are not uncommon. As a founder, you'll tackle whatever needs to be done to achieve your goals. As you start to scale and hire people, you need to figure out how to make sure they are aligned with the company's mission. As Jill pointed out, you want teams to be passionate about your goals, not feel that they are merely cogs in your machine performing a rote task.

So how can you do this?

First of all, it's important to define your company's mission. The top-performing companies have missions to which everyone can align. These are statements that enable leaders to make decisions as to whether a given project aligns with the mission and serves as motivation for employees to know that their efforts are counting toward a great cause. You'll recall that, earlier, we discussed a vision for your company. A vision statement is where you are going. A mission statement is the core philosophy that informs your process and decision-making. It's the reason your company exists, and it will become the reason people want to work with you.

The following are some well-known industry examples:

- Tesla: "To accelerate the world's transition to sustainable energy."
- Google: "To organize the world's information and make it universally accessible and useful."
- Whole Foods: "To nourish people and the planet. We're a purpose-driven company that aims to set the standards of excellence for food retailers. Quality is a state of mind at Whole Foods Market."
- Third Love: "Every woman deserves to feel comfortable and confident."
- Hasbro: "Hasbro is a global play and entertainment company committed to creating the world's best play experiences."

Each of these statements stands on its own. They provide clarity to teams on what is important, and empower individuals and teams to think of new innovative solutions that could help fulfill those missions. For example, what if Tesla's mission was "to make a great electric car"? That would be the end of innovation. Instead, its mission of building a more sustainable energy allows everyone to expand their imagination and cultivate new ideas for the company.

Research shows that innovation happens when teams are able to collaborate and bring diverse experiences and viewpoints to a conversation. As a leader, you need to create a safe place where people are not just rewarded for completing a task, but they are celebrated for carving a new path, forging a new adventure, taking the company to a new level of success because they were inspired by the mission.

You can do this!

Resources That Will Help You Cultivate Team Growth and Development

Table 11.1 summarizes some key resources on innovation and team dynamics that you will find helpful personally and professionally as you expand your business.

These resources should help you gain more insight on how other organizations are thinking about disruption, cultivate a growth mindset in your organization, and understand how to leverage positivity to get what you want from teams.

Table 11.1

Opportunity	Resource/Book
Understand a growth mindset versus A fixed mindset and why it matters in your organization	*Mindset: The New Psychology of Success* by Carol Dweck
Learn to cultivate innovation through diverse viewpoints and research from other organizations	*Resources on Corporate Innovation Strategies:* InnovationLeader.com
Explore appreciative inquiry to improve team dynamics and outcomes	*The Thin Book of Appreciative Inquiry* by Sue Hammond *Appreciative Inquiry: A Positive Revolution in Change* by David L. Cooperrider and Diana Whitney

Chapter 12

The Same Skills That Make You a Great Mom Make You a Great Manager

Bust Out Your Multitasking Skills as Your Team Grows

What you'll take away from this chapter:

In this chapter, we'll explore the ways in which your work as a dedicated caregiver actually makes you better, not less, prepared for formal management and leadership roles. As noted in the introduction, concepts such as mind-minded parenting (which Elizabeth Means coined) focus on having parents work to describe the intentions for the infant in her or his care. This focus builds social bonds, but also helps the infant to develop a better pattern of the world. If we take this type of conscious parenting into the corporate world, we will have leaders who tune in to the needs and goals of their employees, while staying focused on the outcomes needed for success. Just a parent needs to know that the child is making progress toward basic life skills, the employer needs to ensure that the employee is making progress toward goals that benefit the organization.

Sophie's Day

Sophie's day started at 5 a.m. She typically woke up an hour before her kids did so she could have some time for meditation, journaling, and exercise. She had a schedule posted on the refrigerator door. Printed neatly on a chart were lunchtime, snack time, doctor's appointments, local fundraisers, the nutritional needs of the kids, and upcoming trips.

Her husband Jake typically woke up around 6 a.m., grabbed some coffee, showered, and headed out the door to his office by 7 a.m.

Sophie was just finishing her morning Pilates routine when Jake came into the living room.

"Hey Soph, I'm headed to work. Have a great day—love you." He reached over to give her a hug while balancing his full coffeecup.

"Love you too." Sophie looked up, wishing he had another moment to talk before he headed to the office.

"Hey—any big plans today?" Jake knew she was spending some of her day working on the new business idea she'd been talking about.

"Yeah—after I get the kids to their morning activities, I'm actually meeting with a potential client.'

Although Sophie admired Maria's decision to launch a scalable enterprise, she had decided to start her own business with a consultative approach, which she thought would be the right one for her. Even so, as things were getting more real and she was lining up customers, she still struggled with confidence.

"I'm actually really nervous about it. I've been planning all of this for so long, and now that I might actually have a big client beyond some of the smaller local ones … I don't know—I guess I feel like I've been out of the workforce for so long that they won't take me seriously."

"You can't think that way." Jake wondered how much of this Sophie deeply believed, and how much of this conversation was just her way of talking things through.

"What do you mean, I can't think that way! That's how I'm thinking."

"Okay … " Jake put his coffee and bag down. "I can be a few minutes late. Let's talk a sec … We made this decision together that you were going to stay home with the kids, and we made this decision together that you were starting your own business.

"You're the most competent person I know. You've juggled the kids, medical issues, a home renovation."

"But no cares about that … People just assume I'm brain-dead now."

"No matter what job you have, someone's going to assume it's easier than theirs. That's what people do. Look, go to any company and you'll hear people talk about how much easier someone else's job is. But that's the thing—when people are good at something, they make it look easy to everyone else. Professional sports players don't make it look hard to play; that's why it's enjoyable to watch. But of course it's hard. You know and I know that what you've been doing is really challenging, but you've made it look easy. You've been caring for and managing a team of people right here in this house, who become completely unreasonable if a meal is late or they've had too much sugar. You're going to be able to apply those same skills to your new business and will absolutely crush it. In fact, you already are. Those smaller customers you've been working with are legit. Don't let the big name you're about to meet with frighten you. You've seen far worse with some little humans in this house!" Sophie smiled as Jake said this, and thought of how she had handled the last set of tantrums.

"Sophie—you can do this." Jake gave her another hug and headed out the door.

* * *

Managing the Small Corporation of Your Family

In 2019, I started a podcast that focused on sharing more stories of the nuanced paths that careers can take as women navigate career and family. I did this in an effort to shed more light on what's possible. While 43% of women step away from the workforce for a variety of reasons, it's easy to pit one idea, opting in or opting out, against the other and to build cases for why one route is the "right" one. As women who have stepped away look to reenter the workforce, they often have to fight the perception that they were just taking a break. Many women returning to work face a significant pay cut from where they were when they left. Others enter at a lower point on the career ladder and feel that they have to prove themselves again to accelerate their progress.

While there are many resources that are designed to be helpful for women seeking to reenter the traditional workforce,

I'd like to make a case for why that seems unnecessary. Assuming that they kept a particular vertical skill, such as accounting, programming, web design or strategy, up to date, why should they have to reenter at a lower point? If a man were to take time off because he had a sudden financial windfall, he might reenter the workforce at a higher place on the ladder because he and those around him would assume that he was highly successful. Surely he didn't lose any skills while he lounged on a sandy beach somewhere. However, when a woman takes time away from the workforce to manage her family, she is often perceived as unambitious and has to take a step down. I have seen this dynamic play out consistently over my career, and I know it's not right that this happens.

When we send a message that someone needs to start at a lower point on the totem pole because they were parenting, we're essentially saying that that role is easy and lacks value. I understand why people have been conditioned to think this way. If you are working a traditional 40-hour week, and you get a vacation with your family, it's easy to think that this is how it must be all of the time. But the reality is that when you are managing a family with young children, you're dealing with logistics, nutritional requirements, doctors' appointments, testing services, group dynamics, and personalized education. In short, you're managing your family and handling the personal development of humans. You are a manager, and that skill should be recognized as such. It's not a break from work at all.

But going back to my earlier point, I've met many men over the years who approached me with a high level of confidence, eager to explain how they did so well financially at their last job that they were able to take a sabbatical. Their attitudes conveyed a strong sense of confidence, and I rarely asked exactly what they did on their "breaks." I typically felt it was none of my business, and I went back to getting an understanding of how they could help me in the present. In contrast, I've interviewed many women who spent time explaining away their years as a primary caregiver, as if it were something for which to apologize.

Being a Mom Is Being a Manager

What I've learned in the past 15 years is that the skills that competent mothers (or caregivers) use translate very well to management.

When you take on the role of manager within a large corporation, some of your responsibilities include:

1. Building a budget and ensuring that you track to it.
2. Hiring and developing the right people to achieve the outcomes you want.
3. Proactively creating the environment in which people will be their most productive.
4. Positively and quickly reacting to stressful situations that arise (someone is out sick, the software that was delivered has a bug that is causing issues, a customer is angry that they didn't get what they wanted, and so on).
5. Celebrating the success of people on your team.
6. Cultivating a growth mindset in employees and helping them navigate their long-term career development.

Now let's compare those skills to the role of a mom (or primary caregiver) as a manager:

7. Building a budget and ensuring that you track to it.
8. Caring for and developing the people in your home to create the best outcomes for all of them over the course of a lifetime.
9. Proactively creating the environment in which people will be their most able to learn.
10. Positively and quickly reacting to stressful situations that arise (someone threw up on you, someone fell down the stairs, someone ate soap, someone is struggling with reading comprehension).
11. Celebrating the successes and hard work of everyone.
12. Cultivating a growth mindset so that your children go on to be lifelong learners.

We have common stereotypes out there that women are multi-taskers and that moms in particular are good at it. But the reality is that moms are good at dealing with reacting to multiple situations at once. That same skill does translate to management. An article in the *Washington Post* recently described Speaker of the House Nancy Pelosi's transition from full-time parenting to politics. "There was no master plan to develop skills that would later be useful in politics. It just happened, day in and day out, as she toiled in the experience that she saw—and still sees—as the most exciting, exhausting, and important work of her life . . . ." The article went on to describe how Pelosi credits that chapter of her life with making her into the leader she became and how she "hopes that society will begin to view parenting as a 'gold star' on any professional resume." I think the reason many people jump to debate this is because any person can have a child with no qualifications or testing in place. In fact, a young teenager can get pregnant and have a child. Does having a child make one a good manager? Of course not. It's not the act of having a child that lends itself to management. It's the relentless pursuit of maintaining a positive environment where learning, safety, and development can occur that translates to management. So the work becomes for men and women who serve as primary caregivers to document those attributes and skills, so they can share what they did that translates into the world of work.

Dismissing the Guilt of Being a Stay-at-Home Mom

So it's no wonder that women walk around with a huge sense of guilt and a "damned if you do, damned if you don't" mindset when it comes to staying home with children or leaving to go earn a livable wage. While we as a society spend a great deal of time revering motherhood, as Magsamun called out, we don't actually value it. Early childhood caregivers and educators are paid substantially less than their counterparts in K–12 education. At the same time, daycare still has costs that are out of reach for many working families. The system is basically designed to discourage women from heading back to work, and at the same time penalizes them when they attempt to do so. There's also research to suggest that once a professional field moves from being primarily filled with women to primarily filled by men, wages do increase. For example, the first computer programmers were women. The first people to deliver babies were also women. Once men jumped into computer programming and became ob-gyns, wages rose.

Arlie Hochschild's seminal book *The Commercialization of Intimate Life* covers the way in which we as a society will pay for some things but not others. The irony is that no one pays childcare providers enough to make the field a really competitive one that all top performers would like to aspire to, like the medical or legal professions, but it's just expensive enough to make it a burden on families to pay for.

So while there are many resources out there on how to reenter the workforce, if you've been inclined to take a step out for childcare, I'd like to first remind you that caring for young children should not be viewed as time wasted. In fact, you've tackled some of the hardest challenges that managers encounter.

You've managed schedules, allotting time for key activities like reading, snacking, physical activity, and rest. You've provided resources for them to be creative and develop their own projects. You've ensured that they learn how to regulate their own behavior. You've dealt with power struggles.

How Your Two-Year-Old Honed Your Management Skills Like No Other

Have you ever tried to reason with a two-year-old? Have you ever found yourself eye-to-eye with a person who is not even half your size, engaged in a powerful battle of the wills? People have referred to this age as the "terrible twos" because developmentally it's typically the stage when humans start to realize that they can have different viewpoints than their caregiver's. They learn the word "no" and realize that it's incredibly powerful. As a parent, you can deal with this stage by recognizing that this will to argue stems from a desire to feel autonomous and powerful. So it's recommended that you should try to give your two-year-old as many choices as you can rather than simply reminding them that you're in charge. By making their own choices, they can claim some power without being at odds with you, the caregiver.

This same mindset and technique work really well with any group of people. In corporations, the person spreading rumors of layoffs is often the person who feels the most powerless. The person who says "no" in a committee meeting is likely doing so because "no" makes them powerful. So what strategies can you use to make those people feel powerful so that they don't disrupt meetings or cause negative gossip? You can leverage the skills you learned as a mom to manage the situation.

You can do this!

Mom versus Manager

They say once a mom, always a mom, and that often extends to the business world. You keep an eye on your charges' long-term development, you coordinate schedules and you make sure the day-to-day operations remain on track. Table 12.1 gives you a side-by-side comparison that you can leverage when you return to the workforce.

Table 12.1   Comparison of Mom and Management Core Skills

Mom Skill	Management Skill
Instilling a growth mindset in children	Instilling a growth mindset in employees
Mastering calendars for multiple household members	Mastering calendars for multiple employees and stakeholders
Responding to emergencies and unplanned disruptions to the days' plans	Responding to emergencies and unplanned disruptions to the days' plans
Waking in the middle of the night to respond to the cries of a child	Waking in the middle of the night to respond to the crisis of a customer
Managing a budget, ensuring that your family has long-term growing assets, a low amount of debt, and enough cash to meet needs	Managing a budget, ensuring that your company or team has long-term growing assets, a low amount of debt, and enough cash to meet needs

Women Helping Women

You don't have to feel like you're on your own when you're trying to juggle family life and a startup business. The resources in Table 12.2 can help.

Table 12.2 Resources to Help Moms in Business

Resource	Purpose
MomsCanCo (https://www.momscan.co)	A nonprofit focused on helping women develop coding skills
Moms-Running (https://www.moms-running .com)	A company focused on helping women enter politics to ensure proper representation
MOR (https://morismore.com)	A consulting firm offering best practices inclusion practices
Chairman Mom (https://www.chairmanmom .com)	A community site for women (and moms) to share experiences and advice with no ads
The Cru (https://findyourcru.com)	A site founded by writer Tiffany Dufu, focused on helping women find their network of support
Pepperlane (https://home.pepperlane.co)	A company formed to help women launch microbusinesses and find support, where motherhood is an asset
Apres (https://apresgroup.com)	Focused on helping women return to work
LeaderMom (https://www.leadermom.com)	A site designed to offer content, resources, and connection for working moms

Chapter 13

You Are More Than Your Product or Company

Protecting Egos When Things Change

What you'll take away from this chapter:

In this chapter, we'll explore the ways in which ego can impact your work for the worse. We'll dig into some of the ways you can spot ego rearing its head, and find ways to diffuse fear as you move quickly to adapt to changing customer needs.

Letting Go to Move Forward

The feedback from one of the Enterprise clients was telling them to expand their offering. In fact, the data was showing that the new product they launched may not have been the best solution.

"Hannah—we need to rethink this latest offering. We might even need to scrap it and look at other options." Maria had the sales figures and usage data in front of her.

Hannah was feeling a little resistant and uneasy.

"I think what we made is working, and that this customer is asking for something we don't need to deliver." Hannah crossed her arms as she spoke.

"You can't think that way. This is the product we're selling today—but we listen if the market shifts. If our customer needs shift, we'll do something different. The salespeople are saying they can't sell this."

"Well, maybe we need different salespeople." Hannah knew the quiver in her voice betrayed her emotion, but she had just spent countless weeks getting this product to market, and couldn't believe she was about to undo it all.

Maria noticed anger and fear in Hannah's eyes as she spoke. Maria softened her tone and took a different direction.

"Listen, we're here to build this company, and to make sure we're working toward the company mission. I learned that the hard way with help from Jill earlier this year. If this new product isn't getting us there, it's better to have it fail fast than to double down on it. But Hannah. This isn't about you, or your job. You led the team to build the solution we agreed upon. And you did it on time and on budget. We can scrap a project without scrapping you." Maria was serious.

"Thanks for clarifying that, Maria. I guess I felt like I put so much of myself into the product that if it failed, I failed."

"Don't feel that way. This may be your project, but it's just one thing you've made. It's not you. It doesn't define you or your work. Honestly, the issue is that you've got your ego wrapped up in this." Maria shifted to coach Hannah more personally.

"To really do this right, and build this business, we all need to be egoless, meaning we act without fear.

* * *

Diffusing Fear and Creating Psychological Safety

So what does it mean to live without ego? Well, it's not really possible. We all bring our ego to situations at times. But what you can do is learn to discourage it, and identify it when it's happening. The goal of tackling issues where egos arise is to diffuse, redirect, and move on.

Here's a quick example.

At one point I was running a project that required cross-functional support. Overall, co-workers were on board. But one person started hollering—detailing all the reasons this would never, ever work. (Did I mention that he was hollering?) He was actually implying that we were being reckless to suggest it.

His truly irate attitude had other people from other departments nodding to go along with him. Many people would simply prefer a calm resolution than continue an argument. The reality is that once you have established your startup company into a revenue-producing machine, people can get more and more locked into their current roles and responsibilities. It's important to understand that even with concerted efforts to establish a growth mindset and foster innovation, people can still be naturally frightened of change.

In this particular situation, once this person had finished his tirade, I remembered something an executive coach and therapist had taught me many years earlier. When someone is reacting strongly, with emotion and not logic, they are most likely afraid. She had described it to me as watching a giant red balloon inflate. As the tirade grew, the balloon was filling with more and more hot air. But just as that noise draws the attention, it's the moment to see how small the self-worth of the person creating the balloon is. When people feel threatened, they react with flight or fight, which, in the corporate world, can look like blocking a project, putting down those around him or her, or becoming more and more grandiose to describe oneself.

So your job, as you work to manage and lead a team, becomes to gently let the air out of the balloon. The job is to diffuse the ego. And you do that by being very calm and by listening. You avoid a reaction. You listen. You acknowledge and address all of their concerns, and then you let them come to the conclusion on their own.

Or perhaps when you really listen to their small voice, you might learn that there was an element of truth in what they were saying. With either scenario, what's important is not the specific outcome that matters—it's how you manage and diffuse the swelling ego that has the potential to disrupt your team dynamics.

As you work to create psychological safety among your teams, it's important to understand that worry and excitement are actually very similar. While worry and fear are rooted in the persistent belief that something negative might happen in the future, excitement is rooted in the persistent belief that something positive might happen in the future. Helping teams recognize the similarities between the two emotional states can help individuals control their thinking and focus on the outcomes that will make the business more successful.

You can do this!

Important Vocabulary for Navigating Change

Some basic terms to be aware of as you manage teams:

Ego: A person's sense of self-esteem or self-importance.

Pivot: The act of turning around a point. In business, it is the act of moving from one business model to another based on data.

Fear: Simply the unpleasant feeling associated with a potentially bad event in the future.

Excitement: The positive feeling of looking into the future.

Chapter 14

Balance Life at High Speeds

Make Time for Yourself

What you'll take away from this chapter:

In this chapter, we'll explore the ways in which a startup can be all-consuming and can lead to burnout. We'll dig into ways to identify burnout and rethink what balance can look like as you work to build your business and the life you want.

Running on Fumes

Maria felt like she was running on empty. Since she took the funding, she was working around the clock to make the business succeed, but it didn't seem to be helping morale.

"Maria, can I have a frank conversation with you?" Hannah was tiptoeing on the subject a bit.

Maria looked up, surprised. "Of course." Hannah had really become a trusted confidante in the business, and Maria welcomed her feedback.

"No, really. I need to know that I'm talking to you as the friend from the neighborhood rather than one of your first hires right now." Hannah felt the need to set this boundary and make it clear.

"Okay . . . " Maria wondered where this was going. Hannah hadn't usually had trouble talking to her about work situations as they arose, so she wondered why Hannah was being cautious now.

Hannah hesitated for a moment, and then just said what she was thinking. "You look godawful."

"Come again?" Maria was taken aback, as she automatically rubbed her lower eyelids wondering, if her eyeliner was smudged, and wiped her mouth, imagining there might be some leftover lunch lurking there.

"It's not your makeup." Hannah quickly reacted to Maria's response. "I know you're going to make this company a success. We're all here working on that, too ... But what you're doing isn't sustainable, and it's impacting the team; more importantly, it's impacting you." Hannah's tone was sympathetic but direct.

"How am I impacting the team by working hard?" Maria felt defensive and, as she checked herself, she realized she also felt exhausted.

"By skipping lunch ... by being here before everyone else and leaving well after they leave, you're setting a pace that people can't keep up with, and I don't think it's what you set out to do when you started this company. In fact, I don't think people *want* to keep up your pace." Hannah knew *she* didn't.

"I hadn't thought about it that way." Maria started to feel introspective. "I thought I was setting a positive example."

"A positive example starts by you taking care of yourself. You know that instruction that you have to put on your own oxygen mask first? Well, yours is locked tightly in the overhead, and we can see you struggling to breathe. You're completely out of balance." Hannah felt more assured of her critique as she said it, confident that she was helping more than hurting.

"Well, hold on, I have a certain amount of time that I'm here. I have a certain amount of time I dedicate to other personal activities. Isn't that balanced?" Maria was thinking out loud.

"No—balance isn't about splitting up your time 50/50, it's about achieving equilibrium so you can move forward even more quickly," Hannah explained.

"Balance starts with taking care of yourself, mentally and physically."

Maria sat back to process what Hannah was saying.

"You've done it. You've built the business, you raised capital, you're growing the business ... but this isn't a sprint. It's a marathon, and we need to you to be in it for the last mile."

"Well, what do you recommend?" Maria was more focused on the outcomes than on herself, but understood Hannah's point.

* * *

My Story (and Cautionary Tale)

What Hannah felt comfortable bringing up to Maria is something common to entrepreneurs. Because entrepreneurs are essentially out on their own, working to build something from nothing, it's easy for the effort to become all-consuming. When you're breaking away from the 9-to-5 world by creating your own world, you can quickly actually find yourself in a 9-to-9 world or more. This is not because the customers or your company require it. It's because when you're passionate about a project, you can make it all-consuming. And for entrepreneurs in particular, the challenges are difficult because when you're presenting your business to investors and customers, you're focused on telling the best, most positive story. When you turn to your initial employees to sell the company vision, you're focused on that same positive story. So if anything doesn't go incredibly well, it can feel very lonely.

A year or so into my entrepreneurial journey, I thought I had it all under control. I was "balancing" life at home with my kids while I was working on my startup and my husband was at his full-time day job. I had put the kids down for their afternoon quiet time, and laid down on the couch for a moment to gather my thoughts before getting on email. But as I lay there, trying to relax, I realized I couldn't feel my fingers. They were numb and tingling. I sat up to self-assess and realized I could barely feel my thighs. My breath was shortening, and I wasn't sure what was happening.

I managed to pull myself off the couch, with my body tingling, thinking I was having a stroke or heart attack, and I called my doctor.

"Hi, something's not right. I can't feel my fingers or my thighs, and I'm having trouble breathing." I waited for his response, assuming I was headed to the doctor's office.

Instead his voice was calm. Completely calm. Disturbingly calm. It was the same tone I used with the kids when they were out of control.

"I think you're okay. But you may be having a panic attack." He delivered news I had never expected.

"What? No, that's not right. I don't have any issues with anxiety. Something's actually wrong with me." I was convinced something was wrong and that this doctor was just brushing aside my concerns.

"Okay." He was excruciatingly calm. "Let's get you to come in."

And then, just after he said that, I started to feel better ... and realized that I was definitely not experiencing a serious condition. After a trip to the doctor's office, and a full run-through, the diagnosis was that I needed to go see a therapist for anxiety.

I realized through multiple sessions with the therapist, who was also a certified executive coach, that I was simply out of balance. In one of her early assessments, she asked me what I liked to do outside of work, and all I could think of was that I liked to hang out with my family or read. In short, my life had become so singularly focused on achieving my goals while taking good care of my family that I was not really taking good care of myself.

After several conversations, I learned that I also needed to include more of my own creative interests in the day. For me that meant making time to exercise, taking flight lessons, drawing more ... in short, doing more things that gave me joy apart from my work or family pursuits.

I'm not alone in this experience. Studies show that entrepreneurs have higher incidents of emotional distress. This is in part because the initial entrepreneurial journey is a lonely one. As a founder, you are working to maintain your positive vision for clients, for investors, and for employees, and yet behind the scenes you may have real doubts or concerns. So find the things that spark joy in your day apart from your company, and look for ways to network with other founders. Knowing you are not alone and finding creative outlets are both positive ways to move your business and life forward.

What Balance Really Means

Balance is needed to ride a bike and to drive a standard car. It doesn't mean that you consciously lean to one side or the other. It means that you are putting the right pressure on either side so that you can move forward.

The concept of personal balance and professional balance isn't as simple. Depending on the realities of the day, balance might look like having to travel for a week for a conference or taking a week off to spend time with your family. It might mean that you need to address self-care, as I had to, and take the time to do the activities that bring joy and creativity to your life beyond family or work. For some that could be painting, music, or simply challenging exercise.

There isn't a simple recipe for balance and no outcome where you can say, "In a week with 168 hours, I spent 56 hours on work, 56 hours on my family, and 56 hours caring for myself—therefore, I'm in balance!" More like riding a bike, it's about feeling yourself going forward and being cognizant of when you're leaning too far to one side or the other. It's about making slight adjustments in your mental and physical state to keep moving forward.

It's about taking care of you.

You really can do this.

Additional Resources to Avoid Burnout

When you think you just can't make another decision or handle another crisis, turn to one of these resources.

Books for Helping to Think Through Your Needs, Leadership Style, and Time Management

168 Hours: You Have More Time Than You Think, by Laura Vanderkam

Happier Now: How to Stop Chasing Perfection and Embrace Everyday Moments, Even the Difficult Ones by Nataly Kogan

Do More Faster, by David Cohen and Brad Feld, Theme 7, "Work–Life Balance"

Reboot, by Jerry Colonna

Tips to Reduce the Potential for Burnout

- Take a 15-minute break from your device every 90 minutes.
- Encourage walks.
- Introduce morning meditation.
- Encourage journaling in meetings. Provide notebooks and pens.
- While we all love candy, load your office with fresh fruits and vegetables.
- Praise healthy behavior. Encourage employees who are participating in races, taking their lunch break to go to the gym, and so on.
- Check to make sure everyone is taking their vacation time. Check in with people who aren't. As a leader, make sure you take your vacation as well.

Conclusion: You Really Can Start Up and Scale a Business

You Might Just Change the Rules in the Process

What you'll take away from this chapter:

In this chapter, we'll find out what happens to each of the characters and provide some closing thoughts on what a future can look like where more women start companies and build the lives they want, taking full advantage of the opportunities that capitalism affords all of us in a democratic nation.

Sophie and Jake

"Thanks again for your business. It's been a pleasure working with you." Sophie hung up the phone as she settled in to watch her elementary-aged children play soccer. Jake glanced over as he heard her end the call and eased back into the lawn chair he had brought to sit on the sidelines at the local game. "Good meeting?" He grinned.

"Yeah—I can't believe how far this business has grown, but here were are at the game, doing what we always wanted while the bank account is growing. Pretty awesome, right?" Sophie took a moment to breathe in the fall air and scan the field for the kids.

"Yeah, pretty awesome."

"I can't think of another way that I could be closing out work calls and still finding time to do the things I want to do with my family."

"Yeah—it's as if you leapt right over so many of the steps people take, and you landed in the leadership position everyone dreams about. But you landed right here with us and the kids."

"Yeah—I guess I leaned in by starting up," Sophie said with a smile.

"I knew you could do it," Jake said.

Hannah and Stan

"You know, joining Starboard has given me experiences I don't think I ever would have had at Company X"' Hannah reflected on what the last year had been like as she caught up with Stan.

"Yeah—I can't believe all the experiences you've had, and that VP title isn't too shabby either." Stan missed having a trusted friend at work, but was happy for Hannah.

"Yeah—I think if I ever reentered the more mainstream workforce, I wouldn't accept a lower position again."

"Right on ... with all the experiences you've had, anyone would be lucky to have you join their team. In fact, I'd be pretty psyched to work on your team. Starboard is really crushing it."

"Well, we'll see what happens. How's Allen?

"Oh, you know, pretty much the same. But since you left, he's been working with HR to figure out better inclusion practices, and to make sure promotions are more equitable."

"That's encouraging to hear. I had to learn a great deal to advocate more for myself, and earlier on. But it's comforting to know that Allen's working on what he could have done better also."

"Yeah—at the end of the day, companies are trying to retain talent. And you were doing a great job. So he's got to think about how to retain people like you, rather than losing you to a startup down the street ... "

"Yeah, its nice to know that he knows others can do it too ... "

Maria and Jill

"I think I see the NASDAQ in your future, Maria." Jill actually felt that Maria had learned so much in the past year that she was beyond her ability to coach.

"Really—actually, you know what? I can see that too ... " Maria stopped herself from downplaying, and took a breath as she instead imagined the ring of the bell.

"You almost did it." Jill caught Maria in her moment of self-deprecation.

"Right—! I almost feigned disbelief, but I do know I can do it…that *we* can do it…that we *did it* by starting up." Jill's face lit up in confidence as she took stock of what she'd built in the past year.

* * *

How Will You Start Up?

The startup life isn't for everyone. But if you've read through this book, you've learned that it might be the right choice for you to build the life you want. Your options range from creating a private consultancy, opening a brick-and-mortar, or becoming CEO of a company with massive potential for scale. Perhaps you'll join a fledgling startup as an early hire. However you do it, you now have the fundamental resources to get started.

But as you got to see some of the characters interact, you may have noticed something else. The support they provided to each other was key to all of their successes. And in particular, Jill's willingness to mentor was crucial.

Although Maria could have continued to forge ahead alone, she may not have really developed the ability to describe her vision in a way that would enable her to get funding. Later, when she found herself stretched to her limits, it was her close relationship with Hannah that helped straighten her path and lighten her load. Similarly, Sophie may never have attempted to start her own business if Maria hadn't talked to her about what was possible and shared the documents that were necessary to start up.

And I'd be remiss not to mention the impact that male mentors had as well. Sophie was equally encouraged by her husband Jake, and Hannah had a peer mentor in her co-worker Stan. While he got the promotion she wanted, he helped her understand the steps he took to get it. She used those lessons when she left to join Maria's company.

The point in all of these mentoring relationships is to help demonstrate that while the entrepreneurial journey can be lonely, if you surround yourself with the right people, it can be much easier to move quickly, find your path, and chart the course that works best for your life.

Overcoming the Scarcity Mindset: There's Enough for All of Us

In *Lean In*, Sandberg recognized the importance of fostering relationships among women to support each other via mentorship. However, in *Lean Out*, Orr calls out another reality some women experience, that of the impact of the scarcity mindset and competition that can brew among women.

When women were slowly being allowed into the corporate arena, there was often just one or two—the token woman. Being the token woman makes it harder for the woman in that position to find trusted mentors and alliances. It also raises the potential for competition, not between men and women, but between women and other women. In fact, when a member of any underrepresented group manages to enter the traditional establishment, there is often a response from those in power, who seem to say, "Okay, that's enough. You showed you could do it." Take, for example, Senate Majority Leader Mitch McConnell's recent comment about how racism was resolved because we have had a black president.

Likewise, as women have entered the corporate arena in leadership positions, the same voices that celebrate those successes inadvertently call attention to what a minority position they hold. While we can all celebrate the individual successes of CEOs like Meg Whitman, it doesn't take much analysis to realize that women make up a very small percentage—6%, to be exact—of Fortune 500 leaders. This scarcity in positions actually fosters an environment where women may feel compelled to compete with each other for what is perceived to be the one slot available. This in turn contributes to a cultural fascination with the idea of a catfight: Pick up any tabloid and you'll find an example of women being portrayed as competing with other women for an arbitrary resource like a man or a role. The spectacle of two women fighting for a sole resource reinforces the notion that women in power are rare. To expand beyond the number of positions the establishment has rationed out would entail competition with men. To keep women fighting actually keeps women down a level from men, in a lower arena. To put it more bluntly, it has women fighting for the scraps.

But when women enter any arena at scale, that competition mindset dissipates, and the competition becomes among the collective group, not the small subset. There is power in numbers. That power was on display in 2016 when millions of women marched in solidarity. And that power can disrupt the existing systems as women claim their right to build their businesses and shape their world.

Valuing Women as Entrepreneurs

Right now, less than 2% of all venture capital goes to women-led companies. I've heard many male investors say that the issue is one of pipeline. There is some truth to this, but it's not as simple as that. In my first year at Techstars, I struggled to understand where to find female founders in my initial pipeline. But after just a small amount of effort and promotion through events geared toward female founders, I saw my pipeline increase exponentially. In my second-year program, 50% of the companies I accepted had a female founder. Were there suddenly that many more women who started companies? Were they more comfortable applying because they saw a female managing director? Or did I just notice them more because I am also a woman?

While this book is a manifesto for women to consider entrepreneurship as a way to create a better life and more sustainable future, I think it's also worth acknowledging that Techstars made a strategic decision to bring on more female investors in an effort to help level the playing field and change the stats on venture investing. Based on the progress in my programs and in others run by my female counterparts, I'd say it's working. Even more exciting is the competition I'm starting to see develop among my male colleagues, who are accepting the challenge to fund more female founders and are working to ensure that they are attracting a solid number of female candidates as well. My counterpart in Boston was recently celebrated in *Forbes* for the

gender diversity in his program (https://www.forbes.com/sites/
kendalltucker/2019/04/26/startup-accelerators-contributing-to-
or-working-against-tech-diversity/#2f0c3435a97a). This was a
result of his focused effort to establish a more diversified group,
but also a side effect of the healthy competition created by
issuing a challenge to managing directors to source more female
founders. When challenged, men want to win the competition
as badly as women do, and end up leveling the playing field to
do so.

Just as a college is considered stronger by a diverse student
body with an even mix of male and female classmates, so too might
an investor's portfolio. A recent report from McKinsey cited that
the "companies in the top quartile for gender or racial and eth-
nic diversity are more likely to have financial returns above their
national industry medians." So this is an area all investors will need
to actually pay attention to. Those stats I highlighted at the beginning of this book—that of all venture funding only 2% goes to
women? That simply can't stay the norm if investors are focused
on returns in their portfolios.

Find, and Later Become, a Mentor

If you are ready to start your own business, it's worth also taking a
look around your local community to see what resources are available to you and what opportunities exist for networking. Look for
programs or opportunities that are actively working to invest and
support female founders. Along the same lines, if you've already
started up and found some success, consider giving back to others
who may not be as far along.

Long before I joined Techstars, I know that much of my success was the result of having positive mentors, including business
colleagues, my husband, former bosses, parents, siblings, and
friends. My mentors were all people on whom I could rely to
share their honest feedback, help make connections, and serve
as sounding boards for ideas.

One of the many reasons I joined Techstars as a managing
director was for the company's dedication to mentoring. While
I had previously been on the startup CEO side of the table and

was later on the operational side of the table in a large organization, joining Techstars provided a unique opportunity to gain experience as an investor and formally help startup CEOs on their entrepreneurial journeys. What Techstars does is help founders move beyond their local network of family and friend mentors and access a broader pool of mentors, with backgrounds ranging from CEO to professor, to truly accelerate their businesses.

Techstars supports community events, many of which focus on women entrepreneurs, around the world. Do a quick search for a Techstars Startup Week or Weekend, and you'll likely find one in your area. We run 50 highly selective accelerators around the world, any of which you can apply to for a chance to gain up to $120,000 in funding along with access to hundreds of mentors and thousands of additional in-network investors. But any managing director is a person who has walked in your shoes and is just as open to connecting you with their networks, many of which are focused on supporting women in tech and women in entrepreneurship. Even if you are not accepted to a program, you'll often make connections that still prove beneficial.

The structures that exist today in corporate America were designed for another era, but they are part of a broader framework that holds within it the promise of opportunity and justice. Our capitalist system should reward the efforts of labor equally, regardless of gender, and the fact that it currently doesn't reveals that women are often a few steps removed from the pure stream of value creation. Entrepreneurship is a path to the source, to the root of the chain, where companies are created, to the forge where the rules are made and can be changed.

Yes. You Really Can Do This.

Bibliography

Brownie Wise (n.d.). PBS, Public Broadcasting Service. http://www.pbs.org/wgbh/americanexperience/features/tupperware-wise/.

Brownie Wise, the brains behind Tupperware (2018). New England Historical Society (December) 26. http://www.newenglandhistoricalsociety.com/brownie-wise-brain-behind-tupperware/.

Scott Adams affirmations (2016). Mind Hacks. http://mindhacks.org/scott-adams-affirmations/135.

Acker, A. (2016). One little change in how you talk to your kids can help them be more successful. *Upworthy* (January 14). http://www.upworthy.com/one-little-change-in-how-you-talk-to-your-kids-can-help-them-be-more-successful.

Agarwal, P. (2018). Not very likeable: here is how bias is affecting women leaders. *Forbes* (October 24). https://www.forbes.com/sites/pragyaagarwaleurope/2018/10/23/not-very-likeable-here-is-how-bias-is-affecting-women-leaders/#6b475f1f295f.

Amadeo, K. (2019). How diversity at work makes more money for you. *The Balance* (August 20). https://www.thebalance.com/cultural-diversity-3306201.

American Express (2018). Number of women-owned businesses increased nearly 3,000% since 1972, according to new research. Press release (August 21). https://about.americanexpress.com/press-release/research-insights/number-women-owned-businesses-increased-nearly-3000-1972-according.

Amit, A. (2016). The 31 benefits of gratitude you didn't know about: how gratitude can change your life. Happier Human. http://happierhuman.com/benefits-of-gratitude/.

Anderson, E. (2013). How feeling grateful can make you more successful. *Forbes* (November 27). https://www.forbes.com/sites/erikaandersen/2013/11/27/how-feeling-grateful-can-make-you-more-successful/#79d6e0e2de7a.

Applerouth, J. (2017). Troubling gender gaps in education (August 15). https://www.applerouth.com/blog/2017/08/15/troubling-gender-gaps-in-education/.

Applico (n.d.). Platform innovation archives. https://www.applicoinc.com/category/platform-innovation/.

Barron, B. (2017). 9 powerful professional organizations for women in business. *GoDaddy* (March 9). https://www.godaddy.com/garage/9-powerful-professional-organizations-for-women-in-business/.

Basu, T. (2016). How the inventor of Liquid Paper, Bette Nesmith Graham, helped launch MTV. *Mental Floss* (February 26). http://mentalfloss.com/article/76038/retrobituaries-how-inventor-liquid-paper-bette-nesmith-graham-helped-launch-mtv.

Beck, M. and Schenker-Wicki, A. (2013). Cooperating with external partners: the importance of diversity for innovation performance. University of Zurich business working paper no. 331 (March 5). https://www.zora.uzh.ch/id/eprint/174259/1/WPS_3315.pdf.

Beddoes, K., Schimpf, C.M., and Pawley, A.L. (2013). Engaging Foucault to better understand underrepresentation of female STEM faculty. Paper presented at the 2013 ASEE Annual Conference, Atlanta, GA.

Brownie Wise (2019). Wikipedia, Wikimedia Foundation (September 15). https://en.wikipedia.org/wiki/Brownie_Wise.

Bui, Q. and Miller, C.C. (2018). The age that women have babies: how a aap divides America. *New York Times* (August 4). https://www.nytimes.com/interactive/2018/08/04/upshot/up-birth-age-gap.html.

Chessman, K. (2008). 16 legendary women entrepreneurs. *Entrepreneur* (August 6). https://www.entrepreneur.com/article/217929.

Chiu, A. (2018). Michelle Obama swore when criticizing Sheryl Sandberg's "lean in" mantra, and the Internet lost it. *Washington Post* (December 3). https://www.washingtonpost.com/nation/2018/12/03/michelle-obama-swore-when-criticizing-sheryl-sandbergs-lean-mantra-internet-lost-it/.

Clance, P.R. and Imes, S.A. (1978). The imposter phenomenon in high achieving women: dynamics and therapeutic intervention. *Psychotherapy: Theory, Research & Practice* 15 (3): 241–247. doi:10.1037/h0086006.

Cohen, B. and Feld, B. (2011). *Do More Faster: TechStars Lessons to Accelerate Your Startup.* Hoboken, NJ: Wiley.

Colonna, J. (2019). *Reboot: Leadership and the Art of Growing Up.* New York: HarperCollins.

Cooperrider, D.L. and Whitney, D. (2005). *Appreciative Inquiry: A Positive Revolution in Change.* San Francisco, CA: Berrett-Koehler Publishers.

Devaney, E. (2018). 3 things marketers can learn from the rise of Netflix (and the fall of Blockbuster). *Drift* (August 30). https://www.drift.com/blog/netflix-vs-blockbuster/.

Dewar, G. (2018). Mind-minded parenting: does insightful talk about the mind help chdren bond and learn? *Parenting Science.* https://www.parentingscience.com/mind-minded-parenting.html.

Durkin, E. (2018). Michelle Obama on "leaning in": "Sometimes that shit doesn't work." *The Guardian* (December 3). https://www.theguardian.com/us-news/2018/dec/03/michelle-obama-lean-in-sheryl-sandberg.

Dweck, C. (2006). *Mindset: The New Psychology of Success.* New York: Random House.

Dweck, C. (2016). What having a "Growth Mindset" actually means. *Harvard Business Review* (January 13). https://hbr.org/2016/01/what-having-a-growth-mindset-actually-means.

Emmons, R.A. and McCullough, M.E. (2003). Counting blessings versus burdens: an experimental investigation of gratitude and subjective well-being in daily life. *Journal of Personality and Social Psychology* 84 (2, February): 377–389.

Eswaran, V. (2019). The business case for diversity is now overwhelming. Here's why. *World Economic Forum* (April 29). https://www.weforum.org/agenda/2019/04/business-case-for-diversity-in-the-workplace/.

Fey, T. (2012). *Bossypants.* London: Sphere.

Friedberg, B. (2019). Why smart investors should check out these women-led companies. *The Balance* (June 25). https://www.thebalance.com/why-women-led-companies-are-good-stock-picks-4147472.

Garber, M. (2014). The first bra was made of handkerchiefs. *The Atlantic* (November 3). https://www.theatlantic.com/technology/archive/2014/11/the-first-bra-was-made-of-handkerchiefs/382283/.

Grant, A.M. and Gino, F. (2010). A little thanks goes a long way: explaining why gratitude expressions motivate prosocial behavior. *Journal of Personality and Social Psychology* 98 (6, June): 946–955.

Green, A. (2018). 19 things you might not know were invented by women. *Mental Floss* (March 15). http://mentalfloss.com/article/53164/19-things-you-might-not-know-were-invented-women.

Hammond, S. (2001). *The Thin Book of Appreciative Inquiry*, 2e. Bend, OR: Thin Book Publishing.

Harvard Business Review (2018). Digital transformation is racing ahead and no industry is immune. Sponsor Content from DXC Technology (March 9). https://hbr.org/sponsored/2017/07/digital-transformation-is-racing-ahead-and-no-industry-is-immune-2.

Heilman, M.E. (2002). Description and prescription: how gender stereotypes prevent women's ascent up the organizational ladder. *Journal of Social Issues* (December 17). https://spssi.onlinelibrary.wiley.com.

Hewlett, S.A., Marshall, M., and Sherbin, L. (2013). How diversity can drive innovation. *Harvard Business Review* (December). https://hbr.org/2013/12/how-diversity-can-drive-innovation.

Hochschild, A.R. (1975). Inside the clockwork of male careers. In: *Women and the Power to Change* (ed. F. Howe), 47–80. New York: McGraw-Hill.

Hochschild, A.R. (2007). *The Commercialization of Intimate Life: Notes from Home and Work*. Berkeley: University of California Press.

Hunt, V., Layton, D., and Prince, S. (2015). Why diversity matters. McKinsey & Company (January). https://www.mckinsey.com/business-functions/organization/our-insights/why-diversity-matters.

Ifeanyi, KC. (2018). How Huda Kattan built a multi-million-dollar beauty brand from a blog." *Fast Company* (July 9). https://www.fastcompany.com/90180015/how-huda-kattan-built-a-multi-million-dollar-beauty-brand-from-a-blog.

Innovation Leader (n.d.). Resources on corporate innovation strategies. https://www.innovationleader.com.

Iskold, A. (2016). The perfect investor deck for raising a seed round (September 19). https://alexiskold.net/2015/12/31/the-perfect-investor-deck-for-seed-round/.

Jacob, M.P. (1914). Brassiere. US Patent 1115674A, filed February 12 and granted November 3. https://patents.google.com/patent/US1115674.

Jope, A. (2017). Gender equality is 170 years away. We cannot wait that long. World Economic Forum (January 19). https://www.weforum.org/agenda/2017/01/gender-equality-is-170-years-away-we-cannot-wait-that-long/.

Kogan, N. (2018). *Happier now: how to stop chasing perfection and embrace everyday moments (even the difficult ones)*. Sounds True.

Lambert, N.M. and Fincham, F.D. (2011). Expressing gratitude to a partner leads to more relationship maintenance behavior. *Emotion* 11 (1, February): 52–60.

Livingston, G. and Parker, K. (2019). 8 facts about American dads. *FactTank*, Pew Research (June 12). https://www.pewresearch.org/fact-tank/2019/06/12/fathers-day-facts/.

Lorenzo, R., et al. (2018). How diverse leadership teams boost innovation. *BCG* (January 23). https://www.bcg.com, https://www.bcg.com/en-us/publications/2018/how-diverse-leadership-teams-boost-innovation.aspx.

Lucas, A. (2018). Anatomy of a Fortune 500 CEO. Franchise Opportunities.com (September 21). https://www.franchiseopportunities.com/blog/general-franchise-information/anatomy-fortune-500-ceo.

Manning, J.E. (2018). Membership of the 115th Congress: A profile. *Congressional Research Service* (December 20). https://www.senate.gov/CRSpubs/b8f6293e-c235-40fd-b895-6474d0f8e809.pdf.

Mayer, J.D., Roberts, R.D., and Barsade, S.G. (2008). Human abilities: emotional intelligence. *Annual Review of Psychology* 59 (1): 507–536. doi:10.1146/annurev.psych.59.103006.093646.

McCarthy, E. (2019). "Makes going to work look easy": Decades before she was House speaker, Nancy Pelosi had an even harder job. *Washington Post* (February 12). https://www .washingtonpost.com/lifestyle/style/makes-going-to-work-look-easy-how-being-a-full-time-mom-prepared-nancy-pelosi-for-this-moment/2019/02/12/416cd85e-28bc-11e9-984d-9b8fba003e81_story.html.

McClear, S. (2018). How Huda Kattan turned blogging into a beauty empire. *Allure* (November 7). https://www.allure .com/story/huda-kattan-profile.

Meins, E., Fernyhough, C., Fradley, E., and Tuckey, M. (2009). Rethinking maternal sensitivity: mothers' comments on infants' mental processes predict security of attachment at 12 months. In: *Readings on the Development of Children + Reclaiming Childhood* (ed. M. Gauvain and M. Cole), 139–154. W. H. Freeman & Co.

Miller, C. C. (2018). The U.S. fertility rate is down, yet more women are mothers. *New York Times* (January 18). https:// www.nytimes.com/2018/01/18/upshot/the-us-fertility-rate-is-down-yet-more-women-are-mothers.html.

Mindset Works (2017). Dr. *Dweck's research into growth mindset changed education forever.* https://www.mindsetworks.com/ science/.

Minthe, C. (2015). Interview: the Middle East's beauty mogul Huda Kattan bares all. *Vogue Arabia* (May 13). https://en .vogue.me/archive/legacy/interview-number-one-middle-east-blogger-huda-kattan-bares-all/.

Miss Cellania (2014). An "uplifting" story: the history of the bra. *Neatorama* (March 17). https://www.neatorama.com/2014/ 03/17/An-Uplifting-Story-The-History-of-the-Bra/.

Morin, A. (2014). 7 scientifically proven benefits of gratitude that will motivate you to give thanks year-round. *Forbes* (November 23). https://www.forbes.com/sites/amymorin/2014/ 11/23/7-scientifically-proven-benefits-of-gratitude-that-will-motivate-you-to-give-thanks-year-round/#ff63d06183c0.

Murphy, J. (2016). 5 female inventors who changed life as we know it. *Biography* (June 6). https://www.biography.com/ news/famous-women-inventors-biography.

Nazworth, A. (2012). 10 remarkable women in U.S. business history. *InvestorPlace* (April 12). https://investorplace.com/2012/05/10-remarkable-women-in-business-history/.

Neto, V. (2018). Michelle Obama believes "leaning in" does not always work. *Fortune* (December 2). https://fortune.com/2018/12/02/michelle-obama-lean-in.

Orr, M. (2019). *Lean Out: The Truth About Women, Power, and the Workplace.* New York: HarperCollins Leadership, an imprint of HarperCollins.

Parker, G., Van Alstyne, M.W., and Choudary, S.P. (2017). *Platform Revolution: How Networked Markets Are Transforming the Economy—and How to Make Them Work for You.* W.W. Norton.

Reynolds, M. (2016). Three ways gratitude increases success. *Inc.* (November 14). http://www.inc.com/molly-reynolds/3-ways-gratitude-helps-increase-success.html.

Sandberg, S. and Scovell, N. (2014). *Lean In: Women, Work, and the Will to Lead.* New York: Alfred A. Knopf.

Sansone, R.A. (2010). Gratitude and well being: the benefits of appreciation. *Psychiatry* 7 (11, November): 18–22.

Seifert, K. and Sutton, R. (2009). Student diversity. In: *Educational Psychology*, Chapter 4. Minneapolis: University of Minnesota Open Text Books. https://open.umn.edu/opentextbooks/textbooks/educational-psychology.

Seligman M.E.P. et al. (2005). Positive psychology progress: empirical validation of interventions. *American Psychologist* 60 (1, July–August): 410–421.

Stimmel, G. (2019). 11 proven tips to launching a successful Kickstarter project (in 2019). *ProductHype* (August 21). https://blog.producthype.co/kickstarter-tips-2019/.

Strugatz, R. (2019). Huda Kattan: the Face that built a beauty empire. *The Business of Fashion* (April 24). https://www.businessoffashion.com/articles/beauty/huda-kattan-the-face-that-built-a-beauty-empire.

Tinsley, C.H. and Ely, R.J. (2018). What most people get wrong about men and women. *Harvard Business Review* (May–June).

Tucker, K. (2019). Startup accelerators: contributing to or working against tech diversity? *Forbes* (April 26). https://www.forbes.com/sites/kendalltucker/2019/04/26/startup-accelerators-contributing-to-or-working-against-tech-diversity/#60c933e135a9.

Turner, N. (2013). 10 things that American women could not do before the 1970s. *Ms.* (May 28). https://msmagazine.com/2013/05/28/10-things-that-american-women-could-not-do-before-the-1970s/.

US Legal, Inc. (n.d.). PDA—Historical perspective. https://pregnancydiscriminationact.uslegal.com/pda-historical-perspective/.

Vanderkam, L. (2011). *168 Hours: You Have More Time than You Think.* Portfolio/Penguin..

Vare, E.A. and Ptacek, G. (1970). *Patently Female: From AZT to TV Dinners: Stories of Women Inventors and Their Breakthrough Ideas.* New York: Wiley, Internet Archive. https://archive.org/details/patentlyfemalefr00vare/page/26.

Von Furstenberg, D. (2019). Jennifer Hyman. TIME 100 Most Influential People 2019. *TIME.* https://time.com/collection/100-most-influential-people-2019/5567849/jennifer-hyman/.

Walters, J. (2015). Yahoo CEO Marissa Mayer's minimal maternity leave plan prompts dismay. *The Guardian* (September 2). https://www.theguardian.com/technology/2015/sep/02/yahoo-ceo-marissa-mayer-minimal-maternity-leave-plan-prompts-dismay.

Wamsley, L. (2018). Michelle Obama's take on "Lean In"? "That &#%! Doesn't Work." NPR (December 3). https://www.npr.org/2018/12/03/672898216/michelle-obamas-take-on-lean-in-that-doesn-t-work.

Ward, M. (2016). Being grateful improves your chances of success, studies show. CNBC (November 7). http://www.cnbc./2016/11/04/being-grateful-improves-your-chances-of-success-studies-show.html.

Watson-Smyth, K. (2011). Secret history of Tupperware. *The Independent* (October 23). https://www.independent.co.uk/property/interiors/secret-history-of-tupperware-2100910.html.

Wynne, K. (2018). Michelle Obama tells crowd it's not enough to just lean in: "that s*** doesn't work all the time." *Newsweek* (December 2). https://www.newsweek.com/michelle-obama-shocks-book-tour-crowd-swear-word-1240301

Zambas, J. (2018). The 15 most successful female entrepreneurs in the world. *CareerAddict* (November 16). https://www .careeraddict.com/women-entrepreneurs.

Zimmerman, E. (2016). Survey shows visualizing success works. *Forbes* (January 27). https://www.forbes.com/sites/ eilenezimmerman/2016/01/27/survey-shows-visualizing-success-works/#627f6c08760b.

Zipkin, N. (2017). This introvert founder swears by this management tip. *Entrepreneur* (July 6). https://www.entrepreneur .com/article/296829.

Acknowledgments

This book would not be possible without the support of countless people, both while I was writing it and along the journey I described.

Thank you to Amos Schwartzfarb for first inviting me to share my project with the Techstars authors, and to Christen Thompson Lain and Keith Camhi for your early advocacy.

Thank you to Brad Feld, Jenny Lawton, David Cohen, David Brown, and Jason Thompson for generously welcoming me in, and making it all possible.

Thank you to Peter Birkeland for your thoughtful edits, notes, and conversations along the way. Thank you to Richard Narramore and Vicki Adang, the team at Wiley, for your additional perspectives, edits, and conversations. Thank you to Phanat Nen for your cover design work, and to James Harless for helping to push the designs forward.

Thank you to my sisters, Colleen Nguyen and Jennifer Carella, for consistently encouraging and supporting me over the years, and during this project. Thank you to my parents, Vincent and Maureen Vezza, who were my very first teachers. Thank you to my in-laws, Annie and Richard Reuter, for your daily support and calls. Thank you to my husband, Alex Reuter, for your partnership, encouragement, and feedback. And thank you to Thomas Reuter and Christopher Reuter for cheering me on and providing the inspiration for the book.

Thank you to all of the people who have offered words of encouragement and inspired me along this journey: Shira Atkins, Anna Barber, Victor Carella, Clem Cazalot, Brook Colangelo, Rebecca Corbin, Samantha Elliott, Jenny Fielding, Catherine Flavin, Marty Guay, Cathy Hutchings, Sharon Kan, Jenny Kaplan, Warren Katz, Nataly Kogan, Jim Loree, Jennifer McFadden, Wendy McGrath, Lesa Mitchell, Yan Nguyen, John

O'Leary, Sarah Reuter O'Leary, Hilla Ovil-Brenner, Nic Reuter, Stefanie Reuter, Heidi Rogers, Joanne Hahner Ryan, Zoe Schlag, Erin Sparler, Polly Usborne, Anna Vezza, John Vezza, Linda Wayman, Amy Westervelt, and Max Yoder. Whether you were sharing a passing comment or offering hours of conversation, your words mattered.

Thank you to all of the women who have shared their own stories with me, including Erin McCoy Alarcon, Kimberly Amyouny, Anna Barber, Lisa Bennett, Eula Scott Bynoe, Danielle Davies, Erika Fleig, Leslie Forde, Deirdre Galbo, Jennifer Gefsky, Gretchen Halasi-Kun, Jill Herzig, Erica Hogue, Cameron Huddleston, Sharon Kan, Rielly Karsh, Oon-agh Kelly, Sarah Lacey, Susan Magsamen, Sharifah Niles-Lane, Marissa Orr, Lisa Oz, Erica Peterson, Jane Shauck, Cheryl Toto, Laura Vanderkam, Jessie Wei, Julie Wei, and Linda Zecher.

Thank you to the first investors who took a bet on me.

And thank you to all the founders with whom I am privileged to work.

About the Author

Claudia Reuter is an experienced entrepreneur, and executive who has been recognized by the *Boston Business Journal* as a 2016 Woman to Watch in Science and Technology, and as a Changemaker by *HUBWeek*.

She currently serves as a managing director for Techstars, where she makes investments in startups and helps founders on their entrepreneurial journeys. She is also a member of the board of directors of Lessonly and a member of the advisory board of Greenfig. Prior to joining Techstars, she served as the senior vice president of digital services & labs for Houghton Mifflin Harcourt, and was the co-founder and CEO of SchoolChapters, Inc. A graduate of the University of Vermont, she is also a lifelong learner and has completed additional coursework in web design, corporate innovation, and rhetoric at institutions including the Rhode Island School of Design, MIT Sloane, and Trinity College. She is also a graduate of Lead Boston, an experiential program focused on inclusive leadership.

Passionate about sharing more stories of what's possible for women, she is also the host and creator of the podcast *The 43 Percent*, which is currently produced by Wonder Media. *The 43 Percent* has been featured on Apple's New & Noteworthy list, been selected as an Editor's Choice by Himalaya, and featured on Stitcher and NPROne.

She lives in Brookline, Massachusetts with her husband Alex and their sons Thomas and Christopher, along with their rescue dog Nora.